中外文稀有版本文献

《哲学的贫困》

②

英文版

【德】卡尔·马克思 ○ 著

《哲学的贫困》的出版与传播

（代序）

蒲鲁东的《贫困的哲学》发表于1846年，从恩格斯给马克思的信中可知，马克思迅速做出反应并于1847年1月开始用法文写《哲学的贫困》。1847年4月初，这部著作基本完成并付印。6月15日，马克思为该书作了序言。1847年7月，《哲学的贫困》交卡·格·福格勒出版社在布鲁塞尔出版，共印800册，其中的150册运交给巴黎的出版商弗兰克，因而弗兰克的名字也刊印在《哲学的贫困》的扉页上。在这之后，在马克思的有生之年里，法文版《哲学的贫困》没有再版。

一 《哲学的贫困》在马克思和恩格斯生前及欧美世界的传播

《哲学的贫困》出版不久就产生了实际的影响，恩格斯在1847年9月给马克思写信，告诉他一个消息，即海尔贝格在比利时工人协会的会议上用法语作了一个演说，海尔贝格表示，"工人协会"是他最近几个月来所追求的目标，并且指出，他之所以坚定了这个信念是"有幸读了《哲学的贫困》最后一章"[①]。

[①]《马克思恩格斯全集》第47卷，北京：人民出版社2004年版，第474页。

然而，这部著作最初的发行还有一些波折。在当时，每一本新书出版后，出版社都会给作者一定数量的免费赠书，这样，作者可以将这些免费赠书有选择地赠予有关人士，从而达到宣传或推销的目的。马克思也在《哲学的贫困》出版后制定了一个赠书名单，其中包括路易·勃朗。恩格斯与路易·勃朗的多次接触和交谈过程中发现他并未得到《哲学的贫困》，直到1847年11月13日，恩格斯"才终于出乎意料地知道"①，出版商弗兰克给每本赠书加收15苏②，以致大量的书积压在弗兰克手中，没有及时传播。

《哲学的贫困》法文第一版的印数不多，传播和发行渠道又受到政府的管制，因此总体效果不够理想。1880年，法国的茹尔·盖得的机关报《平等报》编辑部向马克思提出请求，希望可以刊登转载《哲学的贫困》中的几个段落。马克思同意，并专门写了《关于〈哲学的贫困〉》的引言，阐述了重刊此书的历史意义，但是完整的版本也未能再版。马克思生前的这个唯一的版本还曾在俄国传播，他在致库格曼的信中写道，他找不到任何一个地方像俄国那样普及他的一些著作，例如《哲学的贫困》和《政治经济学批判》。实际上，早在19世纪40年代，俄国先进的社会人士和政治活动家就已经熟知科学共产主义创始人的最重要著作，其中包括《哲学的贫困》法文第一版，它出现在彼得拉舍夫斯基派的图书馆里。

1885年1月下旬，经恩格斯审定，伯恩施坦和考茨基合译的《哲学的贫困》德文第一版在斯图加特出版。根据马克思在1876年1月1日送给娜·吴亭娜的一本1847年法文版上的修订，在校订过程中，恩格斯对文本做了许多的修改，加了许多注释。在附录中，恩格斯还收入了几篇相关文章：(1) 马克思《论蒲鲁东》一文，摘自1865年《社会民主党人报》；(2) 1859年柏林出版的马克思《政治经济学批判》的片断，即约翰·格雷提出的劳动货币交换乌托邦一段；(3) 马克思于

---

① 《马克思恩格斯全集》第47卷，北京：人民出版社2004年版，第494页。
② 比利时当时的货币单位。

1848年发表的《关于自由贸易问题的演说》,"这个演说和《哲学的贫困》属于著者的同一个发展时期"①。更为重要的是,恩格斯在为其所作的序言中,通过批判德国崇拜"国家社会主义"的理论家、经济学者洛贝尔图斯,揭示了马克思的经济学说在19世纪40至60年代的创立过程,这使得德文第一版《哲学的贫困》在19世纪80年代更具有现实意义。

一般说来,《哲学的贫困》出版后过了40年才开始真正产生影响。在19世纪60年代,虽然当时有针对德国社会民主党的"非常法",但工人革命运动的政治力量还是增长了。在马克思于1883年逝世后没几天,在哥本哈根举行的社会民主党代表大会的与会者们便决定以无愧于马克思学说创始人的方式来宣传他的学说。此时,除了中央机关报《社会民主党人报》外,理论刊物《新时代》也作为社会民主党的定期刊物开始出版发行。一年后,德国社会民主党在1884年10月举行的国会选举中获得了约550000张选票和24个议席。1883年,恩格斯的著作《社会主义从空想到科学的发展》的德文版发行了,《共产党宣言》出了新德文版,恩格斯最关心的《资本论》第1卷德文第三版也问世了,1884年还出版了恩格斯的著作《家庭、私有制和国家的起源》。这种强大的攻势并没有到此为止。1885年初,由爱德华·伯恩施坦和卡尔·考茨基主持并受到恩格斯关怀的马克思的《哲学的贫困》德文版出版了,只有出了这个德文版,这部著作才获得了世界的承认。随后《资本论》第2卷德文第一版和《反杜林论》第二版出版。其中,马克思的《哲学的贫困》为社会民主党提供了重要的论据,当时,德国社会民主党是国际工人运动中最先进的部分,按照恩格斯的评价,它最懂得在阶级斗争的三个方面,即在经济、政治和理论方面互相配合、互相联系,并有计划地领导阶级斗争。

---

① 《马克思恩格斯文集》第4卷,北京:人民出版社2009年版,第214页。

在《资本论》第 1 卷出版后，洛贝尔图斯著文指责马克思"剽窃"了他，并且"不指明出处"就大量使用了他的著作《关于我们国家经济制度的认识》。实际上，马克思在世时，既没有读过洛贝尔图斯的上述著作，也没有读到他的指责，因而马克思没有对这种无端的指责进行驳斥。马克思逝世后，恩格斯为马克思作了公正的辩护。他对洛贝尔图斯的答复一部分放在《资本论》第 2 卷的序言里，另一部分则放到了《哲学的贫困》的序言中。"没有别的办法，因为这两本书将同时出，而指责是洛贝尔图斯本人十分明确地提出来的。在《资本论》里我得庄严郑重，而在《贫困》的序言里我可以畅所欲言。"① 在《哲学的贫困》的序言中，恩格斯指出，洛贝尔图斯所谓的马克思从他那里借用的思想，英国的经济学家早就表述过，是洛贝尔图斯的"惊人的无知"才造成了他的"肆意诽谤"。1885 年 1 月初，这篇序言就以《马克思和洛贝尔图斯》为题刊登在《新时代》杂志第 1 期上。

马克思的《哲学的贫困》恰恰在当时具有一种马克思从未料到的意义。恩格斯利用这个机会提醒人们参悟马克思的《资本论》，相反，几个月后恩格斯在《资本论》第 2 卷的《序言》中又提醒人们参看马克思的《哲学的贫困》。如果没有马克思主义的主要著作《资本论》自 1867 年以来产生的影响，我们很难想象马克思的《哲学的贫困》会产生什么样的影响；这两者具有不可分割的联系，相互影响。卡尔·考茨基 1886 年在《新时代》上发表的一组文章《〈哲学的贫困〉与〈资本论〉》提醒人们注意这一联系，从中，主要是社会民主党的干部、议员和编辑们得到了重要的指导方针。马克思虽然在 1883 年逝世了，但他的学说却越来越成为工人运动的思想指针，并使一般精神生活革命化了。

在恩格斯逝世前后，《哲学的贫困》又出版了几种译本：1891 年，在西班牙的马德里出版了由梅萨翻译的《哲学的贫困》的修订第一版；

---

① 《马克思恩格斯全集》第 36 卷，北京：人民出版社 1975 年版，第 202 页。

1892年，德文第二版出版；除德文第一版序言外，恩格斯又为其作了一篇简短的序言，纠正原文中两处不准确的地方；1895年，意大利文第一版在博洛尼亚出版。恩格斯逝世后，1896年，马克思的女儿劳拉·拉法格整理的法文版第二版出版，该版也根据马克思送给娜·吴亭娜一书上的修正做了更正。其实，早在1885年恩格斯出版德文第一版时，劳拉·拉法格也正准备出版法文第二版，但是这一版的准备工作拖延了。直到恩格斯逝世以后，这一版才在巴黎出版。1898年，由巴加洛夫翻译的保加利亚文第一版在瓦尔纳出版；1900年，由科维尔奇翻译的英文第一版在伦敦出版；等等。从那时起，《哲学的贫困》被翻译为30多种文字在许多国家出版。以英文版为例，《哲学的贫困》至今已经发行了很多版本并多次再版。

英文版中引用最多、最为权威的版本是1976年出版的《马克思恩格斯全集》第4卷，英文版编者对《哲学的贫困》的基本概括一直影响着英语世界，如"马克思的《哲学的贫困》是成熟的马克思主义的最早著作之一"，"《哲学的贫困》是马克思作为一个经济学家的初次公开露面"，"这是第一次发表的概述马克思经济学理论基本论点的著作，这些论点是形成马克思主义政治经济学的出发点"，"在《哲学的贫困》中，马克思简洁而明确地表达了唯物主义历史观的本质"①，等等诸如此类的判断。

目前为止，欧美世界主要语种均出版了《马克思恩格斯全集》，包括英语、德语、法语、西班牙语、葡萄牙语、塞尔维亚语、波兰语、匈牙利语等，而各种语言的《马克思恩格斯全集》中无一例外均收录了《哲学的贫困》，因此，可以说，《哲学的贫困》是马克思、恩格斯经典著作中在欧美世界普及率最高的著作之一。

---

① *Karl Marx Frederick Engels Collected Works*, Volume 6, pp.7-8.

二 《哲学的贫困》在苏联的传播[①]

十月革命前后,《哲学的贫困》在俄国的普及率极高,从1886年第一个俄译本出现到苏联时期多次重译与再版,无不体现着这部著作对苏联民众的巨大影响,从而间接影响到我国;因此,厘清《哲学的贫困》在十月革命前后的出版历史,对我们在当今时代审视《哲学的贫困》的重要思想,具有不可或缺的启示意义。

1883年8月,第一个俄国马克思主义团体"劳动解放社"在日内瓦成立,它在成立之初随即发出了"关于出版《现代社会主义丛书》的通告",从这时起,马克思恩格斯著作的俄译本就在这套丛书内作为该社的正式出版物发行。一方面,由于该社的译本都在国外出版,且是全文,避开了书报检查制删减的威胁。另一方面,恩格斯给劳动解放社的出版活动提供了大量帮助。所以,劳动解放社的译本是十月革命前期的最优秀的译本。

在1884年3月2日,查苏里奇就致信恩格斯,请求他允许他们将《哲学的贫困》以俄文出版,并希望恩格斯把当时打算为准备付印的该书德文第一版所写的序言寄去,再看看校样提出意见。四天后,恩格斯致信查苏里奇:"《哲学的贫困》俄文译本出版的日子,不论对我或对马克思的女儿们来说,都将是一个节日。不言而喻,我是很愿意把对您也许有用的一切材料提供给您的。我的意见如下:除了德文译本,目前正在巴黎出版一个新的法文版本。我正在为这两个版本写一些注释,我将把注释的全文寄给您。马克思在柏林《社会民主党人报》(1865年)上发表的一篇《论蒲鲁东》的文章,可以用来作为序言,这篇文章差不多完全包括了我们所需要的东西……这篇文章只

[①] 这部分内容参照了姚颖的论文,《〈哲学的贫困〉在马克思恩格斯逝世前后及苏联时期出版史述要》,载《新东方》2009年第12期。

保存下来一份……如果在马克思或我的文稿里找不出第二份（几星期之内我就可以知道），那么您能很容易地通过伯恩施坦弄到一个抄本。我一定要给德文版专门写一篇序言……在我看来，俄国读者对此恐怕是不会感兴趣的，因为我们的冒牌社会主义者还没有渗透到他们当中去。但是，您对这一点会有自己的看法，这篇序言如果您认为有用，您可以自行处理。"① 据此，《哲学的贫困》俄文第一版于1886年在日内瓦出版时，查苏里奇加入了恩格斯为德文第一版写的序言。除此之外，还在附录中刊载了马克思在科隆陪审法庭上的辩护词的片段及《政治经济学批判》的片段。

19世纪后半期的沙皇俄国属于高压统治，严格的书报检查制度禁止一切有关马克思主义的出版物在俄国社会中传播，劳动解放社许多的出版物都是用手抄本的形式流传。但是，在19世纪90年代后半期突然出现了一种"非常独特的现象"，"在一个完全没有出版自由的专制制度国家里，在凶恶的政治反动势力对于任何一点政治不满情绪和反抗表示都肆意摧残的时代，革命的马克思主义的理论忽然打开了一条出现于受检查的刊物上的道路，而用来说明这个理论的语言虽然是伊索寓言式的，但终究是一切'感觉兴趣的人'都可以理解的。政府只惯于把（革命的）民意主义的理论当作危险的理论，却照例没有发觉这一理论的内部演变过程，而欢迎一切对这个理论的批评。等到政府醒悟过来的时候，等到书报检察官和宪兵这支笨重的军队终于发觉了新的敌人而加以攻击的时候，已经过去了不少的（照我们俄国的尺度来计算）时间了。在这个时期，马克思主义的书籍一本又一本地出版了，马克思主义的杂志和报纸相继创办起来了，大家都纷纷变成了马克思主义者，人们都来奉承马克思主义者，向马克思主义者献殷勤，出版家因为马克思主义书籍的畅销而兴高采烈"②。正因为如此，1898年，俄国基辅的库什涅列夫协会印刷厂公开出版了《哲学的贫困》第一章的单行本。但为

---

① 《马克思恩格斯全集》第36卷，北京：人民出版社1975年版，第121—122页。
② 《列宁全集》第1卷，北京：人民出版社1972年版，第233页。

了迎合书报检察机关的意旨，书中没有指明作者是谁，并歪曲了马克思有关革命实质的主张。

1899年5月1日，波波夫翻译的《哲学的贫困》被书报检察机关禁止，并且禁止劳动解放社的《哲学的贫困》在俄国的宣传。1901年，贾布利茨基和皮亚京出版社公开出版了由皮亚京和别利亚夫斯基从法文版译过来的《哲学的贫困》完整译本。上面还带有恩格斯的序言，但很快被沙皇政府没收了。书报检察官认为，该书在其现在的形式中，包含了旨在摧毁现存经济制度、国家制度和社会制度的论断，以及对预言无产阶级革命的、社会主义和共产主义的有害学说的宣传。由于国内局势紧张，不断的工人罢工，农民运动和学生运动的加剧，沙皇政府加大了书报检查的力度，1900年至1905年，马克思恩格斯著作不能在俄国公开出版，只能在国外发行，主要在日内瓦。

1905年至1907年，随着国内政治格局的变动，沙皇政府放松了书报检查，允许马克思主义的传播。至此，马克思恩格斯著作大量出版发行，迎来了俄文版传播史上的一次高潮。1905年"启蒙"书籍出版社出版了由乌尔里希翻译的《哲学的贫困》，该书包括恩格斯为德文第一版所作的序言和马克思的《论蒲鲁东》。孟什维克在《知识就是利益》这个期刊的1908年第1、2期上，刊登了《哲学的贫困》《格雷是蒲鲁东的先驱者》《关于自由贸易问题的演说》这几篇文章。1908至1917年，由于1905年革命失败，马克思主义的著作被大量销毁。因此，《哲学的贫困》没有再版。

十月革命胜利以前，人民渴望阅读马克思的政治文献，但当时的条件在客观上制约了马克思恩格斯著作的出版，加上沙俄时期对马克思恩格斯文献的毁灭性的删减。在苏维埃政权建立之初，文献出版的条件极其艰苦，"印刷设备损坏、纸张和油墨缺乏、有经验的出版印刷干部奔赴前线和阵亡"。更为重要的是，此时苏维埃俄国还没有一个统一的马克思学研究和出版中心。马克思恩格斯的著作不仅在莫斯科和彼得格勒的中央出版社出版，而且也在阿尔汉格尔斯克、库尔斯克、基辅、哈尔科夫、雅罗斯拉夫尔、塔什干、伊尔库茨克、明斯克等许多城市出版。由于出版社分散且没有统一的监督，因此只能翻印革命前的马克思恩格斯著作的版本，但好多都是被沙皇政府的书报检察机关删改得不成样子的版本。在当时，《哲学的贫困》就有查苏里奇、皮亚京及别利亚夫斯基、阿列克谢耶夫和乌尔里希几个译本。

1918年，《马克思恩格斯全集》俄文第一版第一次启动。在版本的编排计划中，曾打算第2卷收录《哲学的贫困》。但众所周知，从1918年到1922年的四年内，《马克思恩格斯全集》第一版的第一次启动仅出版了4卷：第3、4、5、6卷。第3卷收录了马克思恩格斯在1848至1849年革命和巴黎公社经验基础上所写的最重要的历史学著作；后3卷则是《资本论》的内容。

为了能集中出版事业，苏维埃人民委员会于1919年5月19日颁布了关于创立国家出版社的法令。沃洛夫斯基被任命为国家出版社的负责人。检查整个共和国范围内的出版活动就属于国家出版社的重要职责之一。为此，国家出版社下设了一个专门委员会，即马克思委员会，检查对马克思恩格斯著作翻译和再版，梁赞诺夫、斯克沃尔佐夫、斯捷潘诺夫、沃尔夫松、梅谢里亚科夫是委员会的成员。这时出版了一些按原文校订过的重要著作的译本，其中就包括《哲学的贫困》。

1920年12月8日，俄共（布）中央全会作出决定，建立世界上第一个马克思主义博物馆；1921年1月11日，根据梁赞诺夫的倡议，俄共（布）组织局决定，这个新的机构改组为马克思恩格斯研究院，使之成为收集、研究和科学发表马克思主义经典作家著作的科学中心。从1923年起，马克思恩格斯研究院展开了出版活动，他们不仅着手出版《马克思恩格斯全集》，还要重新刊印马克思恩格斯某些最重要的著作。1928年，在马克思恩格斯研究院第一任院长梁赞诺夫的主持下，下设在研究院内的国家出版社出版了由维·查苏里奇翻译、普列汉诺夫校订的《哲学的贫困》单行本。梁赞诺夫亲自为其作序。在这个单行本中，不仅收入了恩格斯为德文版第一、二版作的序言，卡尔·马克思的《论蒲鲁东》,还将1846年12月28日马克思致帕·瓦·安年科夫的信作为附录收入。在单行本的末尾还附有详细的注释和人名索引。1929年,该单行本的正文被收入《马克思恩格斯全集》俄文第一版的第5卷中。梁赞诺夫在这卷的"编者序"中指出:"确实,这个译本不是从原文,而是从德文翻译过来的,但我们认真地核对了1847年法文版的原本。……恩格斯为德文版写的序言连同恩格斯在1883至1895年写的其他文章都将收录在第13卷中。"1930年,该单行本再版。

1938年11月14日,联共(布)中央委员会在《关于〈联共(布)党史简明教程〉出版后的宣传工作的决议》中揭露了马克思主义经典作家著作出版中的严重错误。中央委员会要求研究院的工作人员从根本上改革全部工作体系,并指出"清理意识形态部门的疏忽,特别要在马恩列研究院不合格的工作中寻找容许在马克思恩格斯全集翻译成俄语时歪曲和不准确的言辞出现的疏忽"的必要性。决议责成研究院在短期内修正被歪曲的内容,尽快重新出版《马克思恩格斯全集》。因此,从1939年起,开始了苏联出版和发表马克思恩格斯著作的新时期。1939至1940年,苏联马恩列研究院重新出版了一系列马克思恩格斯的著作,包括两卷本的马克思著作选集、《共产党宣言》《社会主义从空想到科学的发展》《雇佣劳动与资本》《工资、价格和利润》《德国农民战争》《法兰西阶级斗争》《费尔巴哈论》《路易·波拿巴的雾月十八日》和《关于共产主义者同盟的历史》等。1941年,新版《哲学的贫困》俄文单行本问世。

1955年,译自法文第一版,并参考了1885年与1892年德文版、1896年法文第二版所作修正的俄文版《哲学的贫困》被收入《马克思恩格斯全集》俄文第二版第4卷。恩格斯为德文第一、二版所作的序言分别被收入《马克思恩格斯全集》俄文第二版的第21、22卷。1956年,苏联国家政治书籍出版社根据《马克思恩格斯全集》俄文第二版的版本出版了《哲学的贫困》单行本,共184页。除正文之外,还包括马恩列研究院所作的说明,恩格斯为德文版第一、二版所作的序言及附录。附录包括 1846 年 12 月 28 日马克思致帕·瓦·安年科夫的信、《关于自由贸易问题的演说》《政治经济学批判》（摘录）以及《论蒲鲁东》四篇文章。从那时起到 1973 年，《哲学的贫困》单行本在苏联曾以 14 种语言出版了 33 次，总印数达到 683000 份。此后，苏联再没有出版过该书的新版本。

三　国内主要版本和传播情况

《哲学的贫困》是马克思主义在中国传播的重要著作之一，是中国人了解的第一批马克思的主要著作之一。《哲学的贫困》在中国的传播对于马克思主义哲学原理的系统化，对于马克思主义中国化的意义和作用是不容忽视的。

（一）新中国成立前的版本与传播

1903 年 2 月 25 日，马君武在日本留学生主办的《译书汇编》杂志上发表了题为《社会主义与进化论比较》一文，在介绍西方的社会主义思想时，马君武提到了马克思，并且第一次用"唯物史观"和"阶级斗争"学说来概括马克思的理论。他虽然对马克思思想的实质还缺乏深邃的洞见，但是他已经充分意识到马克思思想的极端重要性以及对改造旧中国的巨大理论和实践意义。在这篇文章的最后，马君武特意列举了西方著名社会主义思想家的代表著作，在马克思的名下列有《英国工人阶级状况》《哲学的贫困》《共产党宣言》《政治经济学批判》和《资本论》，这也许是中国人第一次通过中文知道这部著作。

1903 年 3 月，维新派开办的上海广智书局出版了赵必振翻译的《近世社会主义》一书，作者是日本人福井准造，这是近代中国较为系统地介绍社会主义学说的第一部译著。书中有"加陆马陆科斯（即卡尔·马克思）及其主义"一章，简要介绍了马克思的生平与活动，其中提到了《哲学的贫困》（当时译作《自哲理上所见之贫困》）的写作过程，而且，《哲学的贫困》中一些重要概念，如"生产力""生产关系""唯物史观""剩余价值""阶级斗争""社会主义"等，已经由日语译为中文，开始形成最初的马克思主义理论的概念体系。

1918年底，李大钊在北京大学组织了马克思主义研究团体，即"马尔克斯学说研究会"，到1920年，研究会已经初具规模并开展经常性的研究活动，特别值得一提的是，在李大钊的建议下，研究会建立了中国第一个马克思主义著作的图书室，命名为"亢慕义斋"，收藏有英文版的《哲学的贫困》，还有《共产党宣言》《雇佣劳动与资本》《路易·波拿巴的雾月十八日》《法兰西内战》等英译本。1919年5月，李大钊在《新青年》"马克思号"专辑中发表了《我的马克思主义观（上）》这一长篇论文。李大钊在文中不仅第一次系统介绍了马克思的学说，而且还通过日本学者河上肇的译文，集中展现了马克思表述唯物史观的主要著作，并且直接引用了《哲学的贫困》中的论述，这是中国人第一次了解到该书的内容，这也是书中内容第一次被译为中文，尽管只有简短的一段话。

他写道：

> 他那历史观的纲要，稍见于一八四七年公刊的《哲学的贫困》，及一八四八年公布的《共产者宣言》。而以一定的公式表出他的历史观，还在那一八五九年他作的那《经济学批评》的序文中。现在把这样著作里包含他那历史观的主要部分，节译于下，以供研究的资料。
>
> （一）见于《哲学的贫困》中的："经济学者蒲鲁东氏，把人类在一定的生产关系之下制造罗纱、麻布、绢布的事情，理解地极其明了。可是这一定的社会关系，也和罗纱、麻布等一样，是人类的生产物，他还没有理解。社会关系与生产力有密切的连络。人类随着获得新生产力，变化其生产方法；又随着变化生产方法，——随着变化他们的生活资料的方法——他们全变化他们的社会关系。

手臼造出有封建诸侯的社会。蒸汽制粉机造出有产业的资本家的社会。而这样顺应他们的物质的生产方法,以建设其社会关系的人类,同时又顺应他们的社会关系,以作出其主义、思想、范畴"①。

另一位热情宣传马克思主义的先驱者陈独秀于 1922 年 5 月 5 日,即马克思诞辰 104 周年之际发表了题为《马克思的两大精神》的一篇短文,陈独秀在文章中谈道:"马克思的唯物史观虽然没有专书,但是他所著的《经济学批判》《共产党宣言》《哲学之贫困》三种书里都曾说明过这项道理。"②

李达也是中国共产党建党之前宣传马克思主义的理论家之一,更是堪称建党初期马克思主义出版事业的主要开创者与奠基人。在 1921 年党的一大上,李达被选为宣传部主任,主管党的宣传出版工作,他还担任中国共产党的第一个党刊,即《共产党》杂志的主编,并参加了《新青年》的编辑工作。1921 年 9 月 1 日,李达在《新青年》第 9 卷第 5 号上登载了《人民出版社通告》,公布了该社当年的出版计划,准备出版"马克思全书"15 种,包括《马克思传》《工钱劳动与资本》《价值价格与利润》《哥达纲领批评》《共产党宣言》《法兰西内战》《资本论入门》《剩余价值论》《经济学批评》《革命与反革命》《自由贸易论》《神圣家族》《犹太人问题》《历史法学派之哲学宣言》与《哲学之贫困》。从"马克思全书"的内容上看,涵盖了马克思主义哲学、政治经济学和科学社会主义三个组成部分。这一出版计划由于历史原因未能及时地落实。

1928 年上海《思想》月刊第 2、3 期上发表了李铁声翻译的《〈哲学底贫困〉底拔萃》,这里节译的是该书的哲学内容的片断。译者是根据日本学者浅野晃编辑的《马克思主义的方法的形成——〈哲学的贫困〉中问题的提出与问题的解决》一书的顺序编辑的,该译本有选择

---

① 参见 1919 年 5 月、11 月《新青年》第 6 卷第 5、6 号上的《我的马克思主义观》。
② 《陈独秀文章选编》,北京:生活·读书·新知三联书店 1984 年版,第 193 页。

地节译了《哲学的贫困》中的部分内容，并添加了标题，文前译者撰写了序言。以译者为第二章拟定的标题为例：

唯物史观底形成

唯物史观

（A）社会底经济形态底发展过程。（近代有产者的生产方法底成立）

（B）社会形态底内的连络底探究，—交互作用与决定要因。对立底均衡。

1. 一般的概括（下层建筑与上层建筑）

2. 经济构造。生产力与生产关系（阶级关系）

3. 物质生产底总过程（生产—交换—分配—消费）与社会的生活过程

4. 法制的，政治的生活过程

5. 意识过程

（C）变革的实践。（人们只在能变革的时候才变革。然而，人们要变革。）

从译者为《哲学的贫困》第二章拟定的标题看，当时的人们已经初步理解并掌握唯物史观的主要观点，即生产力决定生产关系、经济基础决定上层建筑这两对社会基本矛盾的原理，并使之合逻辑地引申出阶级斗争和革命的观点。1929年10月，上海水沫书店出版了杜竹君翻译的《哲学之贫困》，这是第一个中文全译本。书前附德文第一版的序言和德文第二版的按语，书后附录包括《论蒲鲁东》《政治经济学批判》第二章B，即关于货币计量单位的学说，以及《关于自由贸易问题的演说》三篇文章。该版的译者附言写于1929年6月15日。1930年10月，水沫书店再版该书，1946年5月，该版又在作家书屋重印，1947年10月和1949年2月，作家书屋又发行了第二版和第三版。从《政治经济学批判》和《共产党宣言》转向《哲学的贫困》，说明中国共产党对马克思唯物史观译介的视野拓展了。上海亚东图书馆于1930年4月出版了由程始仁编译的《辩证法经典》，该书摘译了八篇马克思和恩格斯关于唯物辩证法的论述，其中包括《哲学的贫困》第二章第一节和第五节的后半部分，篇名为"政治经济学的形而上学"。1930年8月，上海山城书店出版了巴克编译的《社会主义底基础》一书，这是一本文摘性专题集，由《哲学的贫困》等30余篇著述节译组成。

1932年7月，北平东亚书局出版了许德珩翻译的《哲学之贫乏》，该版根据1922年巴黎出版的法文本，同时参阅了1920年美国出版的英文本和日译本，因而是一个更为完善的译本。

许德珩在《我翻译〈哲学之贫乏〉的经过》一文中写道，"我之翻译马克思《哲学之贫乏》一书，是当时某些人宣传无政府主义言论的情况下，针对这股思潮而进行的"，"通过二八运动和争回里大的斗争，使我明确认识到：勤工俭学的理想在当时的社会里是很难实现的。无论是实行工读主义还是勤工俭学主义，都不能达到改造社会的目的，只有在马克思主义的指导下进行社会革命才是唯一的出路。从而增强了我攻读马克思主义经典著作的信心和决心，同时对于无政府主义的一套理论也更加不信任"[①]。1929年秋，上海一家出版社诚邀许德珩翻译马克思的《哲学的贫困》，许德珩欣然接受，他说："我想无政府主义思潮在国内甚是泛滥，马克思的这本书正是批判无政府主义的经典之作，译成中文，亟有必要，于是我就接受了。动手是在这年的十月初。可巧在我翻译了三分之一的时候，一天下午路过上海书店最多的四马路（今为福州路），忽然看见一家书店门口悬着大字广告牌，牌上写着'《哲学之贫困》出版了'。我看了又是欢喜，又是懊悔。欢喜的是，这本书已经出版，令人高兴；懊悔的是我竟然白花费了那些功夫去翻译别人已经出版的书。于是打定主意，决定不再翻译它了。回家来就把这个已经译起

---

① 《马克思恩格斯著作在中国的传播》，北京：人民出版社1983年版，第57、59页。

四万多字的稿子捆束起来，置之高阁，一方面写信给这家书店老板，表示自己愿意放弃这种工作。这本书在当时就如此搁置下来。"① 后来，许德珩发现前译本存在许多问题，于是重下决心继续开始翻译工作。这一译本在马克思主义翻译和传播历史上具有一定意义，在此之后，怎样更准确、更全面、更深刻地把握马克思的唯物史观就成为中国人的一个重要课题。

1942年至1944年期间，何思敬在抗日战争的艰苦条件下，在延安中央党校完成了《哲学的贫困》一书的翻译工作，这一版的主要特点是参照了英文译本，并在译文中增加了"英文版注"。由于抗战后期与解放战争时期的流动性大，这一版直到1949年9月才由解放社出版，11月又在北京、大连、上海等地同时翻印。1950年12月，中国人民大学重印，书前译者注明"教学用书、非卖品"。1953年11月，第二版第3次印刷时改由人民出版社出版，至1972年7月为第二版第7次印刷。

（二）新中国成立后的版本与传播

新中国成立以后，中国共产党高度重视马克思主义经典著作的编译工作，并自1956年起，中央编译局开始陆续出版《马克思恩格斯全集》（中文第一版），并在第4卷中收录了《哲学的贫困》全文，该卷出版于1958年8月。这一版本针对的是普通工人群众，因此，对于一些基本的哲学术语，编译者都利用注释加以说明，如"形而上学"② 概念。

1961年11月，人民出版社发行了未署译者名的单行本，这一版的正文和注释均采用《马克思恩格斯全集》第4卷的译文，恩格斯写的两篇序言是由徐坚新译的，附录中的四篇译文分别采用已出版的马克思著作。1965年9月，该版进行了第11次印刷。另外，1964年10月，

---

① 《马克思恩格斯著作在中国的传播》，北京：人民出版社1983年版，第61页。
② 《马克思恩格斯全集》第4卷，北京：人民出版社1958年版，第138页。

该版还刊行了一种16开大字本，分三册平装。

自20世纪60年代起，中央编译局开始编选《马克思恩格斯选集》，这是中国读者盼望已久的一套书，但是，四卷本的《马克思恩格斯选集》刚刚印好就爆发了"文化大革命"，这些印好的著作只能被尘封在书库里长达6年之久。1971年，周恩来总理主持召开了全国出版工作座谈会，并明确指示要重新编辑出版四卷本《马克思恩格斯选集》。这套书于1972年5月出版，其中节选了《哲学的贫困》第二章中的部分内容。

这期间，依据中共中央编译局的译文，人民出版社还出版了几种《哲学的贫困》的单行本，如1978年版。北京外文出版社根据《马克思恩格斯全集》俄文第二版的文本出版了俄文版《哲学的贫困》单行本，系32开平装本。

改革开放以后，为了满足广大读者的需求，人民出版社于1995年6月出版发行了《马克思恩格斯选集》第二版，1997年5月第3次印刷，印数达到32000册；2004年5月第5次印刷，印数达42000册；2008年11月第7次印刷，印数已达52000册。2009年12月，人民出版社出版刊行了10卷本的《马克思恩格斯文集》，第一卷中节选了《哲学的贫困》第二章的部分内容。2012年出版的《马克思恩格斯选集》第三版中也节选了《哲学的贫困》第二章的部分内容。以上版本与1958年出版的《马克思恩格斯全集》相比，中央编译局在译文上做了较大修改，在注释方面也有较多的增补，而且为读者提供了更多的背景知识。同时，译文中还体现了恩格斯编辑1885年德文版时的修改情况，马克思在送给娜·吴亭娜那本书中所做的修改也体现在注释中。

总之，《哲学的贫困》在中国的传播与中国革命的历程紧密契合，它对于中国人接受马克思主义原理具有重要作用。

（本文来自2013年中央编译出版社出版的姜海波所著《马克思〈哲学的贫困〉研究读本》有关内容。）

THE POVERTY OF PHILOSOPHY

BEING A TRANSLATION OF THE

MISERE DE LA PHILOSOPHIE

(A REPLY TO "LA PHILOSOPHIE DE LA MISERE" OF M. PROUDHON)

BY

KARL MARX

WITH A PREFACE BY

FRIEDRICH ENGELS

Translated by H. Quelch

CHICAGO
CHARLES H. KERR & COMPANY

CONTENTS

Introduction 5
Preface 9
Author's Preface 29
Author's Introductory Note 31

CHAPTER I.—A Scientific Discovery.

Section   I.—Opposition of Utility Value to Exchange Value 33
"   II.—Constituted or Synthetic Value 46
"   III.—Application of the Law of the Proportion of Value—(a) Money 85
"   "   (b) Surplus Labor 97

CHAPTER II.—The Metaphysics of Political Economy.

Section   I.—The Method 112
"   II.—The Division of Labor and Machinery 138
"   III.—Competition and Monopoly 158
"   IV.—Property and Rent 168
"   V.—Strikes and the Combination of Workmen 181

Appendix   I.—Proudhon Judged by Marx 193
"   II.—John Gray and his Theory of Labor Notes 203
"   III.—Free Trade 208

INTRODUCTION.

No apology, I imagine, is necessary for the appearance of this translation of Marx's "Misère de la Philosophie." On the contrary it is strange that it should not have been published in England before, and that the translation of his monumental work, the "Capital," tardy as that was, should have yet been made before that of a work which was originally published some twenty years before "Capital" first appeared.

It may be that the translators and editors of the latter work were of opinion that in view of the comprehensiveness of "Capital," a publication of an English edition of the "Misère de la Philosophie" would be a work of supererogation. Or it may be that they thought a book so distinctly French—as the "Capital" may be said to be distinctly English—and which was, further, exclusively a criticism of a work of Proudhon's little known in England—would have slight interest for English readers. On the other hand, the groundwork of the theories so fully elaborated in "Capital," apart from its exhaustive analysis of the capitalist system of production and distribution, will be found in "Misère." In addition, there are several subjects—notably that of rent—

INTRODUCTION

dealt with in this volume which are barely touched upon in the single book of "Capital" which has been translated into English.

Marx's criticism of Proudhon's theory that "the time which is necessary to create a commodity indicates exactly its degree of utility," so that "the things of which the production costs the least time are the things which are the most immediately useful," has been matched by H. M. Hyndman's crushing refutation of the theory of Final Utility. The subject of rent, too, has been fully dealt with by the latter in the same book, "The Economics of Socialism," published, as the author says, in the hope of furnishing "the rapidly-increasing number of students of sociology with a concise and readable statement of the main theories of the scientific school of political economy founded by Karl Marx and Friedrich Engels." Neither of these facts, however, necessarily detracts from the value of this older work of Marx's. On the question of rent, after reviewing the Ricardian theory and the many objections which present themselves to that theory, Hyndman says: "It seems, therefore, that a wider definition of the rent of land under capitalism is needed than that given by Ricardo, and the following is suggested:— Rent of land is that portion of the total net revenue which is paid to the landlord for the use of plots of land after the average profit on the capital embarked in developing such land has been deducted." On the question of confiscating rent he says it "would not affect the position of the working portion of the community unless the money so obtained were devoted to giving them more amusement, to providing them with better surroundings and the like. . . . In fact, the attack upon competitive rents is merely a capitalist attack. That class sees a considerable income going off to a set of

INTRODUCTION

people who take no part in the direct exploitation of labor; and its representatives are naturally anxious to stop this leakage, as they consider it, and to reduce their own taxation for public purposes by appropriating rent to the service of the State. That is all very well for them."

On this point Marx says: "We can understand such economists as Mill, Cherbulliez, Hilditch and others, demanding that rent should be handed over to the State to be used for the remission of taxation. That is only the frank expression of the hate which the industrial capitalist feels for the landed proprietor, who appears to him as a useless incumbrance, a superfluity in the otherwise harmonious whole of bourgeois production."

"Rent," says Marx, "results from the social relations in which exploitation is carried on. It cannot result from the nature, more or less fixed, more or less durable, of land. Rent proceeds from society and not from the soil."

The criticism of Proudhon's appreciation of gold and silver as the first manifestation of this theory of "constituted value" should be interesting reading to those admirers of the French Anarchist who yet profess their profound detestation of money and its function. So, too, should his declaration against strikes and combinations of workmen. In this we see once more how extremes meet. This declaration of Proudhon's would not be out of place in the organ of the Liberty and Property Defence League.

In this matter of trade union combination, Marx was scarcely accurate in his perception of its development. He clearly did not foresee that the great English trade unions would become fossilised, as it were; and that instead of being a revolutionary force they would become a reactionary mass, opposing the progress of the mere

INTRODUCTION

proletarian outside their ranks, as they have done. With the spread of Socialist ideas among them, however, their exclusive character is being modified, and they may even yet take that place in the revolutionary working-class movement which Marx anticipated they would occupy. Given this change of attitude, the development must inevitably be along the lines he predicted. We are seeing "in face of constantly united capital, the maintenance of the association [becoming] more important and necessary for them than the maintenance of wages," and, further, that the combinations of capital are forcing the trade unions to that point where "association takes a political character."

It is scarcely necessary to point out that in this work, written in 1847, some words have a meaning quite other than that which they bear to-day. Thus, for instance, the words "Socialists" and "Socialism," where they occur, refer to the utopians—who formulated theories of a social system independent of the industrial evolution—and to these theories themselves.

In most cases the numerous quotations have been verified and reproduced in the original. In some instances, however, they are summaries rather than quotations, and appear as translated.

A translation in necessarily an imperfect presentation of the thoughts, ideas, and conclusions of the author. In this work I have endeavored to adhere as closely as possible to the form and letter, as well as the spirit of the original, and to this the indulgent reader is asked to ascribe such faults of language as would otherwise merit his censure.

H. QUELCH.

PREFACE.

THE present work was written in the winter of 1846-7, at a time when Marx had just elucidated the principles of his new historical and economic theory.* The "Système des Contradictions Economique ou Philosophie de la Misère," of Proudhon, which had just appeared, gave him the opportunity of developing his principles in opposing them to the ideas of the man who from then was to take a preponderating place among the French Socialists of his epoch. From the moment when both of them at Paris had lengthily discussed economic questions together, often for whole nights at a stretch, their tendency had been to drift further and further apart: Proudhon's book showed that there was already

---

* "La Misère de la Philosophie," written in French, was published in 1847 in Paris, by A. Franck, 69, Rue Richelieu, and in Brussels by C. G. Vogler, 2, Petite Rue de la Madeline; it was translated into German by E. Bernstein and Karl Kautsky, and published in 1892 by the Social-Democratic Party, together with this preface by Engels.

Marx's own copy of the work, which, as well as his other books were given by his two daughters, Laura and Eleanor, to the German Social-Democratic Party, to form the basis of a library for the party, bears some corrections from the hand of the author. They have been reproduced in this edition.—*Note by Editor.*

PREFACE

an impassable gulf between them; to keep silence was no longer possible. Marx demonstrates in this reply the irreparable rupture which had taken place.

The summary of Marx's judgment of Proudhon is expressed in the article reproduced as an appendix to this work, which first appeared in the *Sozialdemokrat* of Berlin, Nos. 16, 17 and 18. It was the only article Marx ever wrote for that journal. The efforts of Herr von Schweitzer to drag the paper into governmental and feudal waters constrained us to publicly withdraw from it after a few weeks.

The present work has for Germany a special importance which Marx did not foresee. How could he have known that in attacking Proudhon he at the same time struck a blow at the idol of the *Strebars* (arrivistes) of to-day, Rodbertus, whose name even he did not know?

This is not the place to deal at length with the relations existing between Marx and Rodbertus; I may soon have the opportunity to do it. Suffice it here to say that when Rodbertus accuses Marx of having " pillaged " him, and of having in his " Capital " profited much by his work, " Zur Erkenntniss," &c., without making any acknowledgment, he allows himself to be guilty of a calumny which is only to be explained by the natural ill-humor of a misunderstood genius, and his remarkable ignorance of everything occurring outside of Prussia, and notably of Socialist and economic literature. These accusations never, any more than the work we have cited, came under the notice of Marx; of Rodbertus's work he knew nothing, except the three " Sozialen Briefe " (" Social Letters "), and even these certainly not before 1858 or 1859.

There is much more foundation for Rodbertus's claim to have in these letters discovered " the constituted value

PREFACE

of Proudhon" long before Proudhon. But he is wrong in flattering himself with the belief that he was the first to discover it. In any case, the present work criticises him with Proudhon, and this forces me to dilate somewhat upon his fundamental *brochure,* " Zur Erkenntniss unserer Staatswirthschaftlichen Zustände " [On th Explanation of our Economical Position], 1842, at least in so far as this work of his, besides the communism of Weitling, which it also contains, however unconsciously anticipates Proudhon.

In so far as modern Socialism, of no matter what tendency otherwise it may be, proceeds from bourgeois political economy, it almost exclusively attaches itself to the theory of value of Ricardo. The two propositions which Ricardo in 1817 put at the head of his " Principles "; First, that the value of each commodity is only and solely determined by the quantity of labor exacted by its production; and, second, that the product of the totality of social labor is shared between the three classes of landlords (rent), capitalists (profit), and laborers (wages) — these two propositions had already in England afforded material for Socialist conclusions. They had been deduced with so much clearness and profundity that this literature, which has now almost disappeared and which Marx had in great part discovered, could not be surpassed until the appearance of " Capital." We shall return to this another time. When Rodbertus, in 1842, on his side drew certain Socialist conclusions from the principles above stated, that was then certainly an important step for a German to take, but it was only a discovery for Germany. Marx shows how little there is of novelty in a similar application of the theory of Ricardo by Proudhon, who suffered from an equal imagination.

PREFACE

"Whoever is, no matter how little, acquainted with the movement of political economy in England, cannot but know that nearly all the Socialists of that country have, at different times, proposed the *equalitarian* (that is to say, Socialist) application of the Ricardian theory." We might cite to M. Proudhon the "Political Economy" of Hopkins, 1822; William Thompson, "An Inquiry into the Principles of the Distribution of Wealth most Conducive to Human Happiness," 1827; T. R. Edmonds, "Practical Moral and Political Economy," 1828, &c., &c., and we might add pages of "&c." We will content ourselves with hearing an English Communist, Bray, in his remarkable work, "Labor's Wrongs and Labor's Remedy," Leeds, 1839, and these quotations from Bray alone settle, for the most part, the claim to priority set up by Rodbertus.

At this time Marx had not entered the reading-room of the British Museum. Beyond the libraries, besides my books and my extracts, which he read during a journey of six weeks which we made together in England in the summer of 1845, he had perused only the books which one could procure at Manchester. The literature of which we have spoken was then not as inaccessible as it may be at the present time. If, in spite of that, it was unknown to Rodbertus, that is entirely due to the fact that he was an exclusive Prussian. He is the veritable founder of specifically Prussian Socialism, and he is at last recognized as such.

However, even in his beloved Prussia, Rodbertus could not remain in absolute ignorance of the work of others. In 1859 there appeared at Berlin the first book of the "Critique de l'Economie Politique," by Marx. There we find, among the objections raised by the economists against Ricardo, as second objection, p. 40:

PREFACE

"If the value in exchange of a product is equal to the labor time which it contains, the value in exchange of a day of labor is equal to its product. Or, indeed, wages must be equal to the product of labor. But it is the contrary which is true." In a note: "This objection raised against Ricardo from the side of the economists, has been raised again later by the Socialists. The theoretical exactitude of the formula being admitted, the practice is accused of being in contradiction to the theory, and bourgeois society was invited to draw practically the conclusions implied by the theory. Some English Socialists have, at least in this sense, turned the formula of the exchange-value of Ricardo against political economy." We are referred in this note to the "Misère de la Philosophie" of Marx, which was then in all the libraries.

It was, then, sufficiently easy for Rodbertus to convince himself of the real novelty of his discoveries of 1842. Instead of that he has not ceased to proclaim them, and to believe them to be so incomparable that he has never once been able to suppose that Marx all alone could have drawn from Ricardo the same conclusions as Rodbertus himself had done. That was impossible. Marx had "pillaged" him—him to whom the same Marx had offered every facility for convincing himself that long before either of them these conclusions, at least in the gross form that they still possess with Rodbertus, had already been expressed in England.

The most simple Socialist application of the theory of Ricardo is that which we have given above. In many cases it has led to perceptions on the origin and the nature of surplus-value which have gone far beyond Ricardo. The same may be said with regard to Rodbertus. Not only does he in this order of ideas never

PREFACE

present anything which has not already been at least as well said before, but his expositions also possess all the defects of those of his predecessors. He accepts the economic categories of labor, capital, value, in the crude form in which they had been transmitted to him by the economists, under their assumed form, without seeking their content. He thus not only closes to himself all means of developing himself more completely — contrary to Marx who, for the first time, had made something of these propositions so often reproduced during the past sixty-four years — but he takes the road which leads straight to utopia, as we will show.

The above application of the theory of Ricardo, which shows to the workers, that the totality of social production, which is their product, belongs to them because they are the only real producers, leads direct to Communism. But it is also, as Marx shows, false in form, economically speaking, because it is simply an application of morality to economy. According to the laws of bourgeois economy, the greater part of the product does not belong to the workers who have created it. If, then, we say, "That is unjust, it ought not to be"; that has nothing whatever to do with economy, we are only stating that this economic fact is in contradiction to our moral sentiment. That is why Marx has never based upon this his Communist conclusions, but rather upon the necessary overthrow, which is developing itself under our eyes every day, of the capitalist system of production. He contents himself with saying that surplus-value consists of unpaid labor; it is a fact, pure and simple. But that which may be false in form from the economic point of view may yet be exact from the point of view of universal history. If the moral sentiment of the mass regards an economic fact — as, formerly,

PREFACE

slavery and serfdom — as unjust, that proves that this fact itself is a survival; that other economic facts are established thanks to which the first has become insupportable, intolerable. Behind the formal economic inexactitude, may, therefore, be hidden a very real economic content. It would, however, be out of place here to dwell at length on the importance and the history of surplus-value.

We can draw other conclusions from Ricardo's theory of value, and that has been done. The value of commodities is determined by the labor exacted by their production. But it is found that in this wicked world commodities are bought sometimes above, sometimes below, their value, and besides, there is the relation to the variations of competition. As the rate of profit has a tendency to maintain itself at the same level for all capitalists, the price of commodities tends also to sink to the value of labor, through the intermediary of supply and demand. But the rate of profit is calculated upon the total capital employed in an industrial enterprise; on the other hand, in two different branches of industry the annual production may incorporate equal masses of labor, that is to say, present equal values, while, if the wages are at an equal level in these two branches, the capital advanced can be, and often is, doubled or trebled in one or the other branch. Ricardo's law of value, as Ricardo himself has already discovered, is in contradiction to the law of the equality of the rate of profit. If the products of the two branches are sold at their value, the aggregates of profit cannot be equal; but if the rates of profit are equal, the products of the two branches are not sold at their value everywhere and always. We have then, here, a contradiction, an antagonism between two economic laws. The practical solu-

PREFACE

tion operates, according to Ricardo (chap. i., sections 4 and 5) regularly in favor of the rate of profit at the expense of the value.

But Ricardo's definition of value, in spite of its evil characteristics, has a phase which renders it dear to our good bourgeoisie. That is the side on which it appeals with irresistible force to their sense of justice. Justice and equality of rights, those are the twin pillars upon which the bourgeoisie of the eighteenth and nineteenth centuries would raise their social edifice above the ruins of injustice, of feudal inequalities and privileges. The determination of the value of commodities by labor and the free exchange which arises according to this measure of value between the possessors of equal rights, such are, as Marx has already shown, the real foundation upon which all the political, juridical and philosophical ideology of the modern bourgeoisie is erected. When one knows that labor is the measure of commodities, the good sentiments of the worthy bourgeoisie must feel deeply wounded by the wickedness of the world, which, indeed, nominally recognises this principle of justice, but which every moment without compunction actually appears to set it on one side. Above all, the "little man," whose honest labor—even when it is only that of his workmen or of his apprentices—loses every day more and more of its value through the competition of the great industry and of machinery; above all, the small producer must ardently desire a society in which the exchange of products according to their labor-value would be a complete and invariable reality. In other terms, he must ardently desire a society in which a single law of production of commodities reigns fully and exclusively, but in which the conditions which alone render this law effective, that is to say, the other laws of

PREFACE

the production of commodities, or better, of capialist production, were entirely suppressed.

This utopia has struck its roots deep and wide in the thought of the modern middle class—real or ideal. This is demonstrated by the fact that already in 1831 it had been systematically developed by John Gray; that at this period it had been practically tried, theoretically expounded, in England, proclaimed as the most recent truth in 1842 by Rodbertus in Germany, in 1846 by Proudhon in France, and again published by Rodbertus as the solution of the social question, and, so to speak, his social testament in 1871; and in 1884 it receives the adhesion of the sequel evolved under the name of Rodbertus to exploit Prussian State Socialism.

The criticism of this utopia has been made so completely by Marx, as well against Proudhon as against Gray (*Cf.* appendix 2 of this work), that I need only devote myself here to some remarks on the special form that Rodbertus has adapted to formulate and express it.

As we have said: Rodbertus accepts the traditional economic concepts under the exact form in which they have been transmitted to him by the economists. He does not make the slightest attempt to verify them. Value is for him "the quantitative valuation of one thing relatively to others, this valuation being taken for measure." This none too rigorous definition gives us at the most an idea of what value appears almost to be, but does not say absolutely what it is. But as it is all that Rodbertus is able to tell us about value, it is comprehensible that he seeks for a measure of value outside of value. After having at random, and without method, twisted use-value and exchange-value about under a hundred aspects with that power of abstraction so infinitely admired by M. Adolphe Wagner, he arrives at

PREFACE

this result — that there is no real measure of value, and that it is necessary to be content with a supererogatory measure. Labor may be such measure, but only in the case of an exchange between products of equal quantities of labor; if the case is otherwise in other instances, it is not so unless one has taken means to assure it. Value and labor thus remain without the least real relation to each other, although all the first chapter has been devoted to an endeavor to explain to us how and why the cost of commodities is determined by **labor** and by nothing but labor.

Labor is yet again taken in the form in which one meets it with the economists. And not even that. Because although there may be something said as to the difference in intensity of labor, it is very generally represented as something which "costs," that is to say which is a measure of value, whether it be expended or not under the normal conditions of society. Whether the producers employ ten days in the manufacture of products which could be manufactured in one day, or if they employ only one; whether they use the best or the worst implements; whether they apply their labor time to the manufacture of articles socially necessary or in the quantity socially required; whether they make articles for which there is no demand at all or articles for which there is more or less demand — of all that there is no question; labor is labor, the product of equal labor must be exchanged with the product of equal labor. Rodbertus, who in all other cases is always ready, whether it be relevant or not, to place himself at the national point of view and to consider the relations of isolated producers from the height of the observatory of general society, timidly avoids all that here. Simply because from the first line of his book he goes straight to the

PREFACE

utopia of the labor-note, and that all analysis of labor as the producer of value only strews his route with difficulties. His instinct was here considerably stronger than his power of abstraction — that cannot be discovered in Rodbertus, it may be said in passing, only by means of the most concrete poverty of ideas.

The journey to utopia is quickly made. "The dispositions" which fix the exchange of commodities according to the value of labor as following an absolute law present no difficulty. All the other utopians of this tendency, from Gray to Proudhon, are at great pains to elaborate social measures. In order to realize this object they at least endeavor to resolve the economic question by economic means, due to the action of the owner of commodities who exchanges them. For Rodbertus it is much more simple. As a good Prussian he calls in the State. A decree of the public power establishes the reform.

Value is thus then happily "constituted," but not the priority of this constitution which is claimed by Rodbertus. On the contrary, Gray as well as Bray — among many others — have often expressed the same idea; they piously desire measures by which the products will exchange, in spite of all obstacles, always and only at their value in labor. After the State has thus constituted value — at least of a part of the products, as Rodbertus is modest — it issues its labor-notes; in effect, as advances to the industrial capitalists with which the workers are paid; the workers then buy the products with the labor-notes they have received and thus permit the return of the paper money to its original source. It is necessary to learn from Rodbertus himself how admirably that develops.

"For this second condition we must secure the dis-

PREFACE

position which exacts that the value attested should be really in circulation by giving only to him who actually delivers a product, a note on which should be marked exactly the quantity of labor necessary for the manufacture of the product. He who delivers a product of two days' labor would receive a note marked 'two days.' The second condition would be necessarily fulfilled by the strict observance of this regulation in the issue of the notes. According to our hypothesis, the true value of goods coincides with the quantity of labor expended in their manufacture, and this quantity of labor is measured by the division of time expressed. He who delivers a product to which two days' labor have been devoted, if he receives a certificate of two days' labor, has then secured that there should be assigned or certified to him neither more nor less value than he has in fact delivered—and further, as he only who has really put a product in circulation, alone secures such an attestation, it is equally certain that the value inscribed on the note is capable of paying society. Enlarge as much as we will the sphere of the division of labor, if the regulation is properly followed the sum of value disposable must be exactly equal to the sum of value certified, and, as the sum of value certified is exactly the sum assigned, this must necessarily coincide with the value disposable. All the exigencies are satisfied and the liquidation is perfect." (Pages 166, 167.)

If Rodbertus has up to the present had the misfortune of arriving too late with his discoveries, this time, at least, he has obtained a kind of originality; none of his rivals had dared to give to the foolish utopia of the labor-note this form so naïvely infantile, I might even say so truly Pomeranian. Because that for each note an object of corresponding value is delivered, as no object

PREFACE

of value is delivered except against a corresponding note, necessarily the sum of notes is covered by the sum of the objects of value. The calculation is perfectly equal, it is exact to a second of labor time, and there is not a superior employee in the Office of the Public Debt who, however appalled by his own duties, could in this calculation make the slightest error. What more could be desired?

In modern capitalist society each industrial capitalist produces on his own account what he likes, how he likes, and as much as he likes. The quantity socially demanded is for him an unknown magnitude, and he does not know the quality of the objects demanded any more than their quantity. That which to-day cannot be supplied quickly enough may to-morrow be in excess of the demand. Ultimately demand is satisfied in some fashion, ill or well, and generally production is definitely regulated by the objects demanded. How is the reconciliation of this contradiction effected? By competition. And how does that arrive at this solution? Simply by depreciating below their labor value the commodities which are by reason of their quality or quantity useless or unnecessary, in the present state of the demand of society, and in making the producers feel, in this explicit fashion, that they have manufactured articles absolutely useless or unnecessary, or that they have manufactured a superfluity of otherwise useful articles. From that two things follow:

First, the continual deviation of the price of commodities in relation to the value of commodities is the necessary condition by which alone the value of commodities can exist. It is only by the fluctuations of competition, and following that, of the price of commodities, that the law of value realizes itself in the

PREFACE

production of commodities and that the determination of value by the labor time socially necessary becomes a reality. That the form of representation of value, price, has, in general, a quite other aspect than the value which it manifests, is a lot which it shares with the greater part of social relations. The king often bears but slight resemblance to the monarchy which he represents. In a society of producers of exchangeable commodities, to wish to determine value by labor time by interdicting competition from establishing this determination of value in the single form by which it can do this — in influencing its price, is to show, at least in this connection, the habitual utopian misunderstanding of economic laws.

In the second place competition, in realizing the law of value of the production of commodities in a society of producers for exchange, establishes by that means and by assured conditions the single order and the single organisation possible for social production. It is only by the depreciation or appreciation of the price of products that the isolated producers of commodities learn to their cost what kind of things society requires, and the quantity it requires of them. But it is precisely this single regulator which the utopianism shared by Robertus would suppress. And if we ask what guarantee we have that only the necessary quantity of each commodity would be produced, that we should not be wanting corn and meat while there was an abundance of beet sugar and we were inundated with a too plentiful supply of potato spirit, that we should not be lacking breeches to cover our nakedness while breeches buttons were multiplied by the million — Rodbertus triumphantly shows us his famous account, in which there is set forth an exact certificate for each superfluous pound of sugar, for each cask of spirit not purchased, for each useless

PREFACE

breeches button, an account which is "just," which "satisfies all the conditions and in which the liquidation is exact." And anyone who does not believe this has only to address himself to " M. X.," the superior employee of the Office of the Public Debt in Pomerania, who has revised the calculation and has found it just, and who may be regarded as never having been capable of a mistake in his accounts.

And now let us briefly notice the *naïveté* with which Rodbertus would suppress industrial and commercial crises by means of his utopia. When the production of commodities has reached the limits of the world market it is by a cataclysm of this market, by a commercial crisis, that equilibrium is established between the isolated producers, producing each according to his individual calculation, and the market for which they produce, and of the demand of which, both as to quantity and quality, they are ignorant. If competition is to be prevented from making known to the isolated producers the state of the market by the rise or fall of prices, they would be blinded indeed. To direct the production of commodities in such fashion that the producers could not know the state of the market for which they produce — it is to provide for crises in such a fashion as to raise the envy of Doctor Eisenbart for Rodbertus.

We can understand now why Rodbertus determined the value of commodities by labor, and further admitted different degrees of intensity of labor. If he had enquired why and how labor created value and, in consequence, determined and measured it, he would have arrived at socially necessary labor, necessary for the isolated product, as well in relation to other products of the same kind, as well as in relation to the total quantity socially required. He would have been met with the question:

PREFACE

How is the production of isolated producers accommodated to the total social demand? and all his utopia would have become impossible. This time, indeed, he has preferred to abstract, he has made an abstraction of the problem to be solved.

At last we come to the point where Rodbertus offers us something new: the point which distinguishes him from all his numerous comrades of the organisation of exchange by labor-notes. They all acclaim this method of exchange with the object of destroying the exploitation of wage-labor by capital. Each producer must obtain the total labor-value of his product. They are unanimous about this from Gray to Proudhon. Not at all, says Rodbertus, on the contrary. Wage-labor and its exploitation will still exist.

In the first place there is no social state possible in which the laborer could receive for his own consumption the total value of his product. The funds produced must support a number of functions economically unproductive but necessary; and they must consequently maintain the people concerned with these functions. That is true only as regards the present division of labor. In regard to a society where productive labor would be obligatory, a society which is certainly possible, the statement falls to the ground. There still remains the necessity for an accumulated social reserve fund, and then the *laborers,* that is to say *all,* would remain in possession and in enjoyment of the total product, but each isolated worker would not enjoy the integral product of his own labor. The support of functions, economically unproductive, by the product of labor has not been neglected by the other labor-note utopians. But they leave the workers to impose this obligation upon themselves, following in this respect the customary democratic method, while Rod-

PREFACE

bertus, whose whole theory of social reform in 1842 is fashioned according to the Prussian State pattern of that time, refers everything to the judgment of the bureaucracy, which authoritatively determines the share of the worker in the product of his own labor, and graciously abandons that part to him. Then rent and profit must also continue to exist. In fact, the landed proprietors and the industrial capitalists do fulfil certain functions, socially useful, or even necessary, although economically unproductive, and receive in exchange a kind of remuneration, rent and profit—which is a conception scarcely new, even in 1842. Truth to tell, they receive very much too much for the little that they do, and which they do sufficiently ill; but Rodbertus has need of a privileged class, at least for 500 years to come, also the rate of surplus-value, to express myself correctly, that must also exist, but without being capable of being augumented. Rodbertus accepts as the actual aggregate of surplus value, 200 per cent., that is to say, that for a daily labor of twelve hours the worker will not receive a certificate of twelve hours, but one of four hours only, and the value produced in the remaining eight hours must be shared between landlord and capitalist. The labor-notes of Rodbertus lie then, absolutely, but it is necessary to be a Pomeranian feudal proprietor to imagine that there is a working class to whom it would be advantageous to work twelve hours to obtain a labor-note of four hours. If the juggleries of capitalist production were translated in this simple manner, in which it appears as a manifest theft, it would be rendered impossible. Each labor-note given to the worker would be a direct provocation to rebellion, and would fall within the scope of section 110 of the penal code of the German Empire. It is necessary never to have seen any

PREFACE

other proletariat than that of a Pomeranian feudal estate, a proletariat of day laborers, almost serfs, in fact, where the bâton and the whip reign supreme, and where all the pretty girls of the village belong to the harem of their gracious seigneur, to be able to offer such impertinences to the workers. But our conservatives are our greatest revolutionists.

But if the workers were sufficiently simple to allow themselves to be persuaded that having labored for twelve full hours, they have in reality only labored four hours, they would at least be recompensed by being guaranteed that their proportion of the product of their own labor would never fall below a third. That is, in reality, to play the air of the society of the future on a child's trumpet. That is really not worth spending another word upon. Consequently all that Rodbertus offers that is new in his utopia of labor-notes is childish and far inferior to the labor of his numerous rivals, whether they have preceded or followed him.

For the epoch in which it appeared Rodbertus's "Zur Erkenntniss, &c.," was certainly an important book. To pursue the theory of Ricardo in this direction was a promising beginning. If for him and for Germany alone it was a novelty, his work might in its completion have attained the same height as that of the best among his English predecessors. But it was only a commencement of which the theory could only achieve a real result by ulterior, fundamental, critical work. This development was arrested because from the outset the development of the theory of Ricardo was carried in the other direction, in the direction of utopia. From then it lost the essential of all criticism — independence. Rodbertus worked then with a preconceived end; he became an economist with a settled tendency. Once seized by his

PREFACE

utopianism, he is precluded from all possibility of scientific progress. From 1842 until his death he turned in the same circle, reproduced the same ideas, already expressed or indicated in his preceding works, found himself misunderstood, found himself pillaged, when he had nothing of which to be robbed, and at last refused to accept the evidence that at bottom he had discovered nothing which had not already been established long before him.

It is scarcely necessary to remark that in this work the language is not identical with that of "Capital." In this work Marx still speaks of *labor* as a commodity, and of its purchase and sale, instead of *labor power*.

As appendices we have added to this work: 1st, a passage from Marx's work, "Critique de l'Economie Politique," Berlin, 1859, with reference to the first labor-notes utopia of John Gray; and 2nd, the discourse of Marx on "Free Trade" delivered in French at Brussels in 1847, which belongs to the same period of the author's development as the "Misère."

FRIEDRICH ENGELS.

London, October 23, 1884.

AUTHOR'S PREFACE.

M. Proudhon has the misfortune of being singularly misunderstood in Europe. In France he has the right to be a bad economist, because he passes for a good German philosopher. In Germany he has the right to be a bad philosopher, because he passes for one of the greatest of the French economists. We, as both German and economist at the same time, wish to protest against this double error.

The reader will understand that in this ungrateful task it has been often necessary for us to leave the criticism of M. Proudhon, in order to turn to that of German philosophy and to set forth from time to time some views on political economy.

KARL MARX.

Brussels, June 15, 1847.

The work of M. Proudhon is not simply a treatise on political economy, an ordinary book, it is a Bible: "Mysteries," "Secrets dragged from the bosom of God," "Revelations," nothing is wanting. But as, in our days, the prophets are discussed more conscientiously than the profane authors, the reader must resign himself to pass with us by the arid and gloomy erudition of "Genesis" in order to rise later with M. Proudhon into the ethereal and fruitful regions of supra-Socialism. (See Proudhon's "Philosophie de la Misère," Prologue, page 111, line 20.)

THE POVERTY OF PHILOSOPHY

CHAPTER I.
A SCIENTIFIC DISCOVERY.

SECTION I.— OPPOSITION OF UTILITY-VALUE TO EXCHANGE-VALUE.

" The capacity possessed by all products, natural or industrial, to serve the subsistence of man is specially described as *utility-value;* the capacity they have of being given in exchange for each other as *exchange-value.* . . . How does utility-value become exchange-value? . . . The generation of the idea of value (in exchange) has not been noted by the economists with sufficient care; it is important for us to halt here. Since among the objects of which I have need many are found in nature only in very small quantities, or, in some cases, not at all, I am forced to aid in the production of what I want; and, as I cannot turn my hand to so many things, I propose to other men, my collaborators in different functions, to cede to me a portion of their products in *exchange* for mine." (Proudhon, vol 1, chap. II.)

M. Proudhon proposes to himself to, before all, explain to us the double nature of value, *" the distinction in value,"*

THE POVERTY OF PHILOSOPHY

the process which makes exchange-value of utility-value. It is important for us to halt with M. Proudhon at this act of transubstantiation. This is how this act is accomplished according to our author:

A large number of products are not found in nature, they are found at the end of industry. Suppose his needs exceed the spontaneous production of nature, man is forced to have recourse to industrial production. What is this production, in the supposition of M. Proudhon? What is its origin? A single man experiencing the want of a large number of things "cannot turn his hand to so many things." To have so many wants to satisfy supposes so many things to produce—there are no products without production—to have so many things to produce pre-supposes more than the hand of a single man already assisting in production. But from the moment that you suppose more than one hand assisting in production you have already supposed a whole system of production based on the sub-division of labor. Thus the need, such as M. Proudhon supposes it, itself pre-supposes the whole sub-division of labor. In supposing the sub-division of labor you have exchange, and consequently exchange-value. It would have been just as well to have supposed exchange-value in the first place.

But M. Proudhon prefers to make the circuit. Let us follow him in all his detours, to always return to the point of departure.

To leave the state of things in which each produces solitarily, and to arrive at exchange, "I address myself," says M. Proudhon, "to my collaborators in various functions." Then, it seems, I have some collaborators who all have various functions, without I and all the others, in order to arrive at such a state of things— always according to the supposition of M. Proudhon—

A SCIENTIFIC DISCOVERY

having abandoned the solitary and unsocial position of Robinson Crusoe. The collaborators, and the diverse functions, the division of labor and the exchange which it indicates are all existing already.

To summarise: I have wants based upon the division of labor and on the exchange of commodities. In supposing these wants M. Proudhon finds that he has supposed exchange, exchange-value, of which he precisely proposes to "note the generation with more care than the other economists."

M. Proudhon could just as well have inverted the order of things without by so doing inverting the justness of his conclusions. To explain exchange-value there must be exchange. To explain exchange there must be division of labor. To explain the division of labor there must be wants which necessitate the division of labor. To explain these wants it is necessary to *"suppose"* them, which is not to deny them, contrary to the first axiom of M. Proudhon's prologue: "To suppose God is to deny him." (Prologue, p. 1).

How does M. Proudhon, for whom the division of labor is supposed known, take this to explain exchange-value, which for him is always the unknown?

"A man" sets out "to propose to other men, his collaborators in various functions," to establish exchange and to make a distinction between use-value and exchangeable value. In accepting this proposed distinction the collaborators have left to M. Proudhon no other "care" than to take account of the fact, to mark, to "note" in his treatise of political economy "the generation of the idea of value." But he owes it to us, always, to explain "the generation" of this proposition, to tell us, finally, how this single solitary man, this Robinson Crusoe, has had suddenly the idea of making

THE POVERTY OF PHILOSOPHY

" to his collaborators " a proposition of this kind, and how his collaborators have been led to accept it without any protest whatever.

M. Proudhon does not enter into these genealogical details. He simply gives to the fact of exchange a kind of historical *cachet* in presenting it under the form of a motion, which a third party has made, tending to establish exchange.

That is a sample of *" the historical and descriptive method "* of M. Proudhon, who professes a superb disdain for the " historical and descriptive method " of Adam Smith and Ricardo.

Exchange has its own history. It has passed through different phases.

There was a time, as in the Middle Ages, when only the superfluity, the excess of production over consumption, was exchanged.

There was, again, a time when not only the superfluity but all the products, the whole of industrial existence, entered into commerce, in which the whole production depended entirely upon exchange. How are we to explain this second phase of exchange — saleable value at its second power?

M. Proudhon would be prepared with an answer: Admit that a man has *" proposed* to other men, his collaborators in various functions," to raise saleable value to its second power.

Lastly, there comes a time when all that men have regarded as inalienable become objects of exchange, of traffic, and can be disposed of. It is the time in which even the things which until then had been communicated, but never exchanged; given, but never sold; acquired, but never bought — virtue, love, opinion, science, conscience, &c.— where all at last enter into commerce. It

A SCIENTIFIC DISCOVERY

is the period of general corruption; of universal venality, or, to speak in the terms of political economy, the time when everything moral or physical having become a saleable commodity, is conveyed to the market to be appraised at its proper value.

How can we explain this new and last phase of exchange — saleable value at its third power?

M. Proudhon would have an answer all ready: Put it that a person has "*proposed* to some other persons, his collaborators in various functions," to make of virtue, love, &c., a saleable value, to raise exchange-value to its third and last power. We thus see that the "historical and descriptive method" of M. Proudhon suffices for everything, it answers to everything, it explains everything. If it is above all a question of explaining historically "the generation of an economic idea," he supposes a man who proposes to other men, his collaborators in various functions, that they should accomplish this act of generation, and all is said.

Henceforth we accept the "generation" of exchange-value as an accomplished fact; it only remains now to explain the relation of exchange-value to utility-value. Listen to M. Proudhon.

"The economists have very well explained the double character of value; but what they have not set out with equal clearness is its *contradictory nature;* it is here that our criticism begins. . . . It is a small matter to have signalised in utility-value and exchange-value this astonishing contrast, in which the economists are accustomed to see nothing but the most simple matter: it is necessary to show that this pretended simplicity hides a profound mystery which it is our duty to penetrate. . . . In technical terms use-value and exchange-value are in inverse ratio the one to the other."

THE POVERTY OF PHILOSOPHY

If we have grasped M. Proudhon's idea, here are the four points he proposes to establish:

(1) Utility-value and exchange-value form an "astonishing contrast," they are in opposition to each other.

(2) Utiltity-value and exchange-value are in inverse ratio the one to the other, in contradiction.

(3) The economists have neither seen nor known, either the opposition or the contradiction.

(4) The criticism of M. Proudhon begins at the end.

We also, we will commence at the end, and in order to clear the economists from the accusations of M. Proudhon we will hear what two economists of some importance have to say.

Sismondi: "It is the opposition between value in use and exchangeable value to which commerce has reduced all things, &c." ("Études,"," vol. II., p. 162. Brussels edition.)

Lauderdale: "In general national wealth (utility-value) diminishes in proportion as individual fortunes increase by the augmentation of saleable value; and to the extent that these are reduced by the diminution of this value, the first generally increases." ("Enquiries into the Nature and Origin of Public Wealth.")

Upon the opposition between use-value and exchange-value Sismondi has based his principal theory that the diminution of the revenue is in proportion to the increase of production.

Lauderdale has based his system on the theory of the inverse raito of the two kinds of value, and his doctrine was so popular at the time of Ricardo that the latter could speak of it as of a thing generally known:—

"It is through confounding the ideas of value and wealth, or riches, that it has been asserted that by diminishing the quantity of commodities, that is to say,

A SCIENTIFIC DISCOVERY

of the necessaries, conveniences and enjoyments of human life, riches may be increased." (Ricardo, "Principles of Political Economy.")

We have just seen that the economists before M. Proudhon have "signalised" the profound mystery of oppositon and contradiction. Let us now see how in his turn M. Proudhon explains this mystery after the economists.

The exchange-value of a product falls in proportion as the supply increases; in other terms, the greater the abundance of a product *relatively to the demand*, the lower its exchange-value or its price falls. And *vice versa*, the smaller the supply relatively to the demand, the higher the exchange-value or the price of the product rises; in other terms, the geater the scarcity of the products offered relatively to the demand the dearer they are. The exchange-value of a product depends upon its abundance or its scarcity, but always in relation to the demand. Suppose a most rare product, one unique of its kind, if you will: this unique product would be more than abundant if it were not wanted at all. On the other hand, suppose a product multiplied by millions, it will be always scarce so long as it does not meet the demand; that is to say, if it is in too great demand.

These are mere truisms, but it is necessary to reproduce them here in order to make M. Proudhon's mysteries clearly understood.

"Therefore in following the principle to its ultimate consequences we come to this conclusion, the most logical in the world, that the things which are most necessary as articles of use, and whose quantity is infinite can be had for nothing, and those of which the utility is nil and which are extremely scarce will have an inestimable price. To increase the difficulty, actual

THE POVERTY OF PHILOSOPHY

practice does not admit these extremes; on the one side, no human product ever attains the infinite in magnitude; on the other the most scarce things have need of some degree of utility in order to be possessed of any value. Use-value and exchange-value are thus fatally chained to each other, although by their nature they continually tend to exclude each other." (Vol I., p. 39.)

What is it which adds to the difficulty of M. Proudhon? It is simply that he has forgotten the *demand,* and that a thing can only be scarce or abundant according as it is in demand. Demand once set aside he assimilates exchange-value to *scarcity* and use-value to *abundance.* Practically in saying that the things "of which the *utility* is *nil,* and which are *extremely scarce,* will have an *inestimable price,*" he simply says that exchange-value is nothing but scarcity. "Extreme scarcity and utility nil," is pure scarcity. "Inestimable price" is the maximum of exchange-value, it is pure exchange-value. He puts these two terms in equation. Then, exchange-value and scarcity are equivalent terms. In arriving at these pretended "extreme consequences," M. Proudhon finds in effect that he has pushed to extremes, not the things, but the terms which express them, and in that he demonstrates his rhetoric rather than his logic. He finds once more his first hypotheses in all their nakedness when he believes that he has discovered new consequences. Thanks to the same process he succeeds in identifying use-value with pure abundance.

After having put in equation exchange-value and scarcity, utility-value and abundance, M. Proudhon is astonished not to find utility-value in scarcity and exchange-value, nor exchange-value in abundance and utility-value; and in seeing that actual practice does not admit of these extremes he can do no other than believe

A SCIENTIFIC DISCOVERY

in the mystery. There is for him inestimable price, because there are no buyers, and he will never find them while he continues to exclude demand.

From another side, the abundance of M. Proudhon seems to be something spontaneous. He all at once forgets that there are people who produce, and that it is to their interest never to lose sight of the demand. If not, how can M. Proudhon have been able to say that the things which are very useful must be very cheap, or even cost nothing? He ought to have concluded, on the contrary, that it is necessary to restrict abundance, the production of very useful things, if one wished to raise their price, their value in exchange.

The old vine growers of France, in asking for a law prohibiting the planting of fresh vines; the Dutch, in burning the spices of Asia, in uprooting the clove-trees in the Malays, wished simply to reduce abundance in order to raise the exchange-value. So the society of the Middle Ages, in limiting by law the number of associates whom a single master could employ, and in limiting the number of instruments he could use, acted on the same principle. (See Anderson, " History of Commerce.")

After having represented abundance as use-value and scarcity as exchange-value — nothing more easy than to demonstrate that abundance and scarcity are in inverse ratio — M. Proudhon identifies use-value with supply and exchange-value with demand. To make the antithesis still more clear, he substitutes other terms by putting *value of choice* instead of exchange-value. Here then the struggle has changed its ground and we have on one side *utility* (use-value, supply), on the other *choice* (exchange-value, demand).

These two powers opposed the one to the other, who will reconcile them? What can be done to bring them into accord? Is it possible for us only to establish between them a point of comparison?

"Certainly," cries M. Proudhon, "there is one, it is *choice!* The price which will result from this struggle between supply and demand, between utility and choice, will not be the expression of eternal justice."

M. Proudhon proceeds to develop this antithesis:

"In my character of *free purchaser,* I am the judge of what I want, judge of the convenience of the article, judge of the price I am willing to put upon it. On the other hand, in your quality of *free producer,* you are master of the means of production, and in consequence you have the power to reduce your cost of production." (Vol. I., p. 42.)

And as demand, or exchange-value, is identical with opinion, M. Proudhon is led to say:

"It is proved that it is the *free will* of man which gives rise to the opposition between use-value and exchange-value. How can we solve this opposition whilst maintaining free will? And how can we sacrifice this, without at least sacrificing man?" (Vol. I., p. 51.)

Thus then there is no result possible. There is a struggle between two incommensurable powers, so to speak, between utility and choice, between the free purchaser and the free producer.

Let us examine these things a little more closely.

Supply does not represent utility exclusively; demand does not represent choice exclusively. He who demands, does he not also offer a product of some kind, or the representative sign of all products, money; and in supplying this does he not, according to M. Proudhon, represent utility, or use-value?

On the other hand, he who offers, does he not also demand a product of some kind, or the representative sign of all products? And does he not thus become the representative of choice, of the value of choice, or exchange-value?

A demand is at the same time an offer, an offer is at the same time a demand. Thus the antithesis of M. Proudhon in simply identifying supply and demand, the one to utility, the other to choice, rests merely on a futile abstraction.

What M. Proudhon calls value of utility other economists, with as much reason, call value of choice. We will only cite Storch. ("Cours d'Économie Politique," Paris, 1823, pp. 88 and 99.)

According to him, those things are called *wants*, of which we feel the want; those things are called *values* to which we attribute value. Most things only have value because they satisfy wants engendered by choice. Opinion as to our wants may change, then the utility of things, which expresses only the relation of those things to our wants, may change also. Natural wants themselves change continually. What variety there is, for instance, in the objects which serve as the staple food among different peoples!

The struggle is not really between utility and choice; it is between the saleable value demanded by him who wishes to sell, and the saleable value offered by him who makes the demand, who wishes to buy. The exchangeable value of the product is each time the result of these contradictory appreciations.

In a final analysis, supply and demand bring together production and consumption, but production and consumption based upon individual exchanges. The product offered is not utility in itself. It is the consumer who verifies its utility. And even when its quality of utility is recognised, it is not exclusively utility. In the course of production it has been exchanged against all the expenses of production, such as raw material, workpeople's wages, &c., all things which are saleable values. Thus the product represents, in the eyes of the producer, a sum of saleable values. What he offers is not merely an object of utility, but, above all, a saleable value.

As to demand, it can only be effective on condition that it has at its disposal some means of exchange. These means themselves are products, saleable values.

In supply and demand then, we find, on one side a product which has cost some saleable values, and the desire to sell; on the other, some means which have cost some saleable values and the desire to purchase.

M. Proudhon opposes the *free purchaser* to the *free producer*. He has given to the one and to the other some purely metaphysical qualities. This it is which makes him say: "It is proved that it is the free will of man which gives rise to the opposition between use-value and exchange-value."

The producer, from the moment that he has produced in a society based on the division of labor and the exchange of commodities — and that is the hypothesis of M. Proudhon — is forced to sell. M. Proudhon makes the producer master of the means of production; but he will agree with us that it is not upon his free will that his means of production depend. Further, these means of production consist largely of products which come to him from without, and in modern production he is not even free to produce whatever quantity he likes. The actual degree of development of productive forces obliges him to produce on such and such a scale.

The consumer is not more free than the producer. His choice depends upon his means and his wants. The one and the other are determined by his social position,

A SCIENTIFIC DISCOVERY

which itself depends upon the entire social organisation. Thus the worker who buys potatoes, and the kept woman who buys lace, follow the one and the other their respective choice. But the diversity of their choice is explained by the difference in the positions which they occupy in the world, a difference which is the product of the social organisation.

Is the entire range of wants based upon choice or upon the whole organisation of production? In most cases wants spring directly from production or from a state of things based upon production. The commerce of the world almost entirely turns upon wants arising not from individual consumption but from production. Thus, to take another example, does not the need for notaries presuppose a given civil right, which is only an expression of a certain development of property; that is to say, production?

For M. Proudhon it is not sufficient to have eliminated from the relation of supply and demand the elements of which we have just spoken. He pushes abstraction to the farthest limits, in confounding all producers in a single producer, all consumers in a single consumer, and in establishing the struggle between these two chimerical personages. But in the real world matters go otherwise. The competition between those who offer, and the competition between those who demand, forms a necessary element of the struggle between buyers and sellers, from which saleable value arises.

After having eliminated the cost of production and competition, M. Proudhon can at his ease reduce to absurdity the formula of supply and demand.

"Supply and demand," he says, "are nothing but two *ceremonial forms* serving to set before each other use-value and exchange-value, and to effect their reconciliation. They are the two electric poles which, when put into relation with each other, produce the phenomenon of affinity called *exchange*." (Vol. I., pp. 49 and 50.)

This amounts to as much as saying that exchange is only a "ceremonial form" to bring face to face the consumer and the object of consumption. As well say that all economic relations are "ceremonial forms" serving as intermediaries to immediate consumption. Supply and demand are relations of a given production, neither more nor less than are individual exchanges.

Of what, after all, then, does M. Proudhon's dialectic consist? In substituting for use-value and exchange-value, for supply and demand, some abstract and contradictory notions, such as scarcity and abundance, utility and choice, *a* producer and *a* consumer, both of them *chevaliers of free will*.

And to what, as the result of all this, does he come?

To arrange the means of introducing later one of the elements which he had excluded, the *cost of production*, as the synthesis between use-value and exchange-value. It is thus that in his eyes the cost of production constitutes *synthetic value*, or constituted value.

SECTION II.—CONSTITUTED OR SYNTHETIC VALUE.

"Value (saleable) is the corner-stone of the economic edifice." *"Constituted"* value is the corner-stone of the system of economic contradictions.

What then, is this "constituted value" which constitutes all M. Proudhon's discovery in political economy?

Utility being admitted, labor is the source of value. The measure of labor is time. The relative value of products is determined by the labor time it is necessary

A SCIENTIFIC DISCOVERY

to employ in order to produce them. Price is the monetary expression of the relative value of a product. Finally the *constituted* value of a product is simply the value which is constituted by the labor time embodied in it.

Just as Adam Smith discovered the *division of labor,* in the same way M. Proudhon claims to have discovered "constituted value." This is not precisely "something unheard of," but then it must also be admitted that there is nothing unheard of in any discovery in economic science. M. Proudhon, who feels all the importance of his discovery, nevertheless seeks to attenuate its merit, "in order to reassure the reader with regard to his pretensions to originality and to conciliate those whose timidity rendes them but little favorable to new ideas." But, while admitting that each of his predecessors has done something for the appreciation of value, he is compelled to loudly proclaim that it is to him that the greater part, the lion's share, belongs.

"The synthetical idea of value was vaguely perceived by Adam Smith.... But this idea of value was entirely intuitive with Adam Smith; nevertheless, society does not change its habits on the faith of intuitions, it decides only on the authority of facts. It is necessary that the contradiction should be expressed in a clearer and more sensible manner. J. B. Say was its principal exponent."

There is the whole history of the discovery of synthetical value—to Adam Smith vague intuition, to J. B. Say contradiction, to M. Proudhon the constituent and "constituted" truth. And let there be no mistake; all the other economists, from Say to Proudhon, have done nothing but wander in the beaten path of contradiction.

"It is incredible that so many men of sense should for forty years have *struggled* against such a simple idea.

THE POVERTY OF PHILOSOPHY

But no, *the comparison of values is effected without there being any point of comparison between them and without unity of measure*: — that is what *the economists of the nineteenth century,* rather than embrace the revolutionary theory of equality, have resolved to maintain towards and against all. *What will posterity say about it?"* (Vol. I., p. 68.)

Posterity, so brusquely apostrophised, will commence by being puzzled about this chronology. It must necessarily ask: But were not Ricardo and his school economists of the nineteenth century? The system of Ricardo, which set forth the principle " that the relative value of commodities depends exclusively on the quantity of labor required for their production," appeared in 1817. Ricardo is the chief of a whole school which reigned in England since the Restoration. The Ricardian theory sums up, rigorously, pitilessly, all the doctrine of the English middle class, itself the type of the modern bourgeoisie.

"What will posterity say about it?" It will not say that M. Proudhon did not know Ricardo, because he speaks of him, deals with his theory at considerable length, returns to it constantly, and ends by saying that it is rubbish. If ever posterity concerns itself with the subject, it will say, perhaps, that M. Proudhon, fearing to shock the anglophobia of his readers, has preferred to make himself the editor responsible for the ideas of Ricardo. However that may be, it will find it very curious that M. Proudhon gave as a "revolutionary theory of the future" that which Ricardo had scientifically explained as the theory of existing society, of bourgeois society, and that he thus took for the solution of the contradiction between utility and exchange-value what Ricardo and his school had, a long time before him, pre-

A SCIENTIFIC DISCOVERY

sented as the scientific formula of a single side of that contradiction of *exchange-value*. But let us put posterity altogether on one side and confront M. Proudhon with his predecessor Ricardo. Here are some passages from that author which sum up his theory of value.

"It is not utility which is the measure of *exchange-value* although that quality is absolutely necessary." (Vol. I., p. 3, "Principles of Political Economy.")

"Things, once they are recognised as useful in themselves, draw their exchange-value from two sources: from their scarcity and from the quantity of labor necessary to acquire them. There are some things the value of which depends only on their scarcity. No amount of labor being capable of increasing their quantity, their value cannot fall through their too great abundance. Such are rare statues, pictures, &c. This value depends solely on the faculties, the tastes and the caprice of those desirous of possessing such objects." (Vol. I., pp. 4 and 5.) "These, however, form but a very small part of the commodities which are constantly exchanged. The greater number of desirable objects being the fruit of industry, they can be multiplied, not only in one country, but in many, to an extent to which it is almost impossible to fix any limits, every time that one is willing to employ the industry necessary to create them." (Vol. I., p. 5.) "When, then, we speak of commodities, of their exchange-value, and of the principles which regulate their relative price, we have in view only those commodities the quantity of which can be increased by the industry of man, the production of which is encouraged by competition, and is not prevented by any obstacle." (Vol. I., p. 5.)

Ricardo quotes Adam Smith, who, according to him, "has defined with great precision the primitive source

THE POVERTY OF PHILOSOPHY

of all exchange-value" (Vol. I., ch. 5 of Smith), and he adds: "That such must in reality be the basis of exchange-value of all things (namely, labor time) except those which the industry of man cannot multiply at will, is a doctrinal point of the highest importance in political economy; for there is no source from which have flowed so many errors, and out of which have sprung so many diverse opinions in this science as from the vague and indefinite sense attached to the word *value*." (Vol. I., p. 8.)

"If it is the quantity of labor embodied in an article which regulates its exchange-value, it follows that every increase in the quantity of labor must necessarily increase the value of the object upon which it has been employed, in the same way every reduction in the amount of labor must bring about a reduction in price." (Vol. I., p. 9.)

Ricardo afterwards reproaches Smith:

(1) "With having given to value a measure other than labor, sometimes the value of wheat, sometimes the quantity of labor which an article would purchase, &c." (Vol. I., pp. 9 and 10.)

(2) "With having admitted the principle without reserve, and to have, nevertheless, restricted its application to the rude and primitive state of society which preceded the accumulation of capital and the ownership of land." (Vol. I., p. 21.)

Ricardo devotes himself to demonstrating that the ownership of land, that is to say rent, cannot change the relative value of commodities, and that the accumulation of capital exercises only a passing and oscillating influence on the relative values determined by the comparative quantity of labor employed in their production. In support of this proposition he formulates his famous

A SCIENTIFIC DISCOVERY

theory of rent, decomposes capital and comes, in the final analysis, to find that there is nothing but accumulated labor. He afterwards develops a whole theory of wages and profit, and demonstrates that wages and profit rise and fall in inverse ratio the one to the other, without influencing the relative value of the product. He does not ignore the influence which the accumulation of capitals and the difference in their nature (fixed capital and circulating capital), as well as the rate of wages, may exercise on the proportional value of the products. There are, indeed, the principal problems which occupy Ricardo.

"Every economy of labor," says he, "never fails to reduce the relative value of a commodity, whether this economy be effected in the labor necessary to the manufacture of the article itself or in the labor necessary to the formation of the capital employed in that manufacure." (Vol. I., p. 48.) "In consequence, while a day's labor continues to give to one the same quantity of fish and to the other the same of game, the natural rate of the respective prices of exchange will remain the same, whatever may, otherwise, be the variation in wages and in profit, and in spite of all the effects of the accumulation of capital." (Vol. I., p. 32.) "We have regarded labor as the foundation of the value of things, and the quantity of labor necessary to their production as the law which determines the respective quantities of commodities which must be given in exchange for others; but we have not pretended to deny that there may be in the current prices of commodities some accidental and passing deviation from this primitive and natural price." (Vol. I., p. 105). "It is the cost of production which regulates, in the last analysis, the price of things

THE POVERTY OF PHILOSOPHY

and not, as has often been advanced, the proportion between supply and demand." (Vol. II. p. 253.)

Lord Lauderdale had developed the variations of exchange-value according to the law of supply and demand, or of scarcity and abundance relatively to demand. According to him the value of a thing would increase when its quantity diminished or demand increased; it would diminish in proportion to the increase of its quantity or to the reduction of demand. Thus the value of anything might change by the operation of eight different causes, namely, four causes appertaining to the thing itself, and four causes appertaining to money or any other commodity which served as measure of its value. Here is Ricardo's refutation:

"The products of which an individual or a company has the *monopoly* vary in value according to the law which Lord Lauderdale has postulated: they fall in proportion as they are supplied in greater quantity, and they rise with the desire of purchasers to acquire them; their price has no necessary relation to their natural value. But as to the things which are subject to competition between the sellers, and of which the quantity can be increased within reasonable limits, their price depends definitely not upon the state of demand and of supply, but upon the actual cost of production." (Vol. II., p. 159.)

We will leave the reader to compare the precise, clear, and simple language of Ricardo with the rhetorical efforts made by M. Proudhon in order to arrive at the determination of relative value by labor time.

Ricardo shows us the real movement of bourgeois production which constitutes value. M. Proudhon, making abstraction of this movement, "struggles" to invent new processes in order to regulate the world

A SCIENTIFIC DISCOVERY

according to a professedly new formula which is only the theoretical expression of the real existing movement so well expounded by Ricardo. Ricardo takes for his point of departure existing society to demonstrate to us how it constitutes value. M. Proudhon takes for his point of departure constituted value, in order to constitute a new social world by means of this value. For him, M. Proudhon, constituted value must make a circuit and become the constituent for a world already fully constituted according to this mode of valuation. The determination of value by labor time is for Ricardo the law of exchange-value; for M. Proudhon it is the synthesis of use-value and exchange-value. The theory of value of Ricardo is the scientific interpretation of actual economic life; the theory of value of M. Proudhon is the utopian interpretation of the theory of Ricardo. Ricardo proves the truth of his formula by drawing his conclusions from all the economic relations and in explaining by this means all the phenomena, even those which at first sight appear to contradict it, such as rent, the accumulation of capitals, and the connection between wages and profits; that is precisely what makes of his theory a scientific system. M. Proudhon, who has rediscovered this formula of Ricardo's by means of entirely arbitrary hypotheses, is compelled afterwards to seek for isolated economic facts which he tortures and falsifies, in order to make them serve as examples, applications already existing, of the beginnings of the realisation of his regenerating idea. (See our Section 3, " Application of Constituted Value.")

Let us now pass on to the conclusions which M. Proudhon draws from value constituted (by labor time).

— A given quantity of labor equals the product created by the same quantity of labor.

THE POVERTY OF PHILOSOPHY

— Every day's labor is worth another day's labor; that is to say, in equal quantity the labor of one is worth the labor of another: there is no qualitative difference. Given an equal quantity of labor, the product of one will exchange for the product of another. All men are wage-workers, and equal wages pay for an equal time of labor. Perfect equality presides over the exchange.

Are these conclusions the natural, rigorous consequences of value "constituted," or determined, by labor time?

If the relative value of a commodity is determined by the quantity of labor required to produce it, it naturally follows that the relative value of labor, or wages, must be equally determined by the quantity of labor which is necessary to produce the wages. The wage, that is to say the relative value, or price, of labor, is then determined by the labor-time which is necessary to produce all that is required for the subsistence of the worker. *"Reduce the cost of manufacturing* hats and eventually their price will fall to their new natural price, although the demand may be doubled, trebled, or quadrupled. *Reduce the cost of subsistence of men* by reducing the natural price of the necessary food and clothing and you will see wages eventually fall, although the demand for hands may have considerably increased." (Ricardo, vol. II., p. 253.)

Certainly the language of Ricardo is most cynical. To put in the same category the cost of manufacturing hats and the cost of subsistence of man, is to transform man into a hat. The cynicism is in the things themselves, and not in the words which express these things. Some French writers, such as MM. Droz, Blanqui, Rossi and others, give themselves the innocent satisfaction of proving their superiority to the English economists by

A SCIENTIFIC DISCOVERY

seeking to observe the etiquette of "humanitarian" language; if they reproach Ricardo and his school with their cynical language, it is because they are annoyed at seeing economic conditions exposed in all their crudity, at seeing the mysteries of the bourgeoisie betrayed.

Let us sum up: Labor being itself a commodity, measures itself as such by the labor-time necessary to produce this labor-commodity. And what is necessary to produce the labor-commodity? Exactly that amount of labor time which is necessary to produce the objects indispensable to the constant subsistence of labor; that is to say, to enable the workers to live and to propagate his race. The natural price of labor is nothing but the minimum wage. If the current price of wages rises above the natural price it is precisely because the law of value, postulated in principle by M. Proudhon, finds itself counterbalanced by the consequences of the variations in the relation between supply and demand. But the minimum wage is, nevertheless, the centre towards which the current price of wages constantly gravitates.

Thus relative value, measured by labor-time, is fatally the formula of the modern slavery of the worker, instead of being, as M. Proudhon would have it, the "revolutionary theory" of the emancipation of the proletariat.

Let us now see in how many cases the application of labor time as the measure of value is incompatible with the existing antagonism of classes and the unequal distribution of the product between the immediate worker and the possessor of accumulated labor.

Let us suppose a certain product: for instance, linen. This product, as such, embodies a definite quantity of labor. This quantity of labor will be the same no matter what may be the reciprocal positions of those whose labor has combined to create this product.

Let us take another product (cloth) which has **exacted** the same quantity of labor as the linen.

If there is an exchange of these products there is an exchange of equal quantities of labor. In exchanging these equal quantities of labor, we do not change the reciprocal position of the producers any more than we change something in the situation of the workers and manufacturers among them. To say that this exchange of products measured by time has, for its consequence, the equal remuneration of all the producers, is to suppose that equality of participation has existed anterior to the exchange. When the exchange of the cloth for the linen has been accomplished, the producers of the cloth will share in the linen in precisely the same proportions as they before shared in the cloth.

The illusion of M. Proudhon proceeds from his taking as a necessary consequence what at the most can be nothing but a gratuitous assumption.

Let us go further.

Does labor time, as the measure of value, suppose at least that the days are *equivalent,* and that the day of one is worth the day of another? No.

Assuming, for a moment, that the day of a jeweler is worth three days of a weaver, all changes in the value of jewels relatively to the value of woven stuffs must always, apart from the passing effects of the oscillation of supply and demand, have for cause a reduction or an increase on one side or the other of the time employed in production. Let three days of labor of different workers be in the proportion of 1, 2, 3, and all change in the relative value of their products will be a change in this proportion of 1, 2, 3. Thus

A SCIENTIFIC DISCOVERY

value may be measured by labor time in spite of the inequality of value of different days of labor; but, to apply a similar measure it is necessary for us to have a comparative scale of the different days of labor; it is competition which establishes this scale.

Is your hour of labor equal to mine? That is a question debated and settled by competition.

Competition, according to an American economist, determines how many days of simple labor are contained in a day of complex labor. Does not this reduction of days of complex labor to days of simple labor suppose that simple labor is itself taken as the measure of value? The single quantity of labor serving as the measure of value supposes in its turn that simple labor has become the pivot of industry. It supposes that labors are equalised by the subordination of man to the machine, or by the extreme division of labor; that men are effaced before labor; that the balance of the pendulum has become the exact measure of the relative activity of two workers as it is of the speed of two locomotives. Then it is not necessary to say that the hour of one man is worth the hour of another man, but rather that a man of one hour is worth another man of an hour. Time is everything, man is nothing; he is no more than the carcase of time. There is no more question of quality. Quantity alone decides everything, hour for hour, day for day; but this equalisation of labor is not the work of M. Proudhon's "eternal justice"; it is solely the accomplishment of modern industry.

In the automatic workshop the labor of one worker is scarcely distinguished in anything from the labor of another worker: the workers cannot distinguish between themselves except by the quantity of time they work. Nevertheless, this quantitative difference becomes, at a

THE POVERTY OF PHILOSOPHY

certain point of view, qualitative, inasmuch as the time given to work depends, in part, on purely material causes, such as physical constitution, age, and sex; in part on purely negative moral qualities, such as patience, impassability, assiduity. Lastly, if there is a difference of quality in the labor of the workers it is at most a degree of the last quality, which is far from being a distinctive speciality. Such is, in the final analysis, the state of things in modern industry. It is on this already realised equality of automatic labor that M. Proudhon bases his plane of "equalisation" which he proposes to realise universally in "the time to come."

All the "equalitarian" consequences which M. Proudhon draws from the doctrine of Ricardo rest upon a fundamental error. That is, that he confounds the value of commodities measured by the quantity of labor embodied in them with the value of commodities measured by *"the value of labor."* If these two methods of measuring the value of commodities were confounded in one, we might say indifferently, the relative value of any commodity is measured by the quantity of value embodied in it; or, it is measured by the quantity of labor which it is able to purchase; or, again, it is measured by the quantity of labor which will purchase it. It is necessary, indeed, that it should be thus. The value of labor could no more serve as a measure of value than the value of any other commodity. Some examples will serve to more fully explain the above point.

If a quarter of wheat cost two days' labor instead of one, it would have double its primitive value; but it would not put in motion a double quantity of labor, because it would contain no more nutritive matter than before. Thus the value of the wheat, measured by the quantity of labor employed to produce it, would have

A SCIENTIFIC DISCOVERY

doubled; but measured either by the quantity of labor that it could buy, or by the quantity of labor by which it could be bought, it would be far from having doubled. On the other hand, if the same labor produced double the amount of clothing as before, the relative value would fall to one half; but nevertheless this double quantity of clothing will not thereby be reduced to command only half the quantity of labor, nor could the same quantity of labor command double the quantity of clothing, as the half of the clothing would continue to render to the workers the same service as before.

Thus, to determine the relative value of commodities by the value of labor is contrary to economic facts. It is to move in a vicious circle, to determine relative value by a relative value which, in its turn, needs to be determined.

It is beyond doubt that M. Proudhon confounds the two measures, the measure by the labor-time necessary to the production of a commodity, and the measure by the value of the labor. "The labor of every man," says he, "will purchase the labor which it embodies." Thus, according to him, a certain quantity of labor embodied in a product equals in value the remuneration of the worker, that is to say, the value of labor. It is, once more, the same reason which leads him to confound the cost of production with wages.

"What are wages? They are the price of the amount of wheat, &c., ... the integral price of all things." Let us go further still: "Wages are the proportionality of the elements which compose wealth!" What are wages? They are the value of labor.

Adam Smith takes as measures of value, sometimes the labor time necessary to the production of a commodity, sometimes the value of labor. Ricardo exposed

THE POVERTY OF PHILOSOPHY

this error by showing clearly the disparity between these two methods of measuring. M. Proudhon enhances the error of Adam Smith by identifying the two things which the latter had only placed in juxtaposition.

It is in order to find the just proportion in which the workers should share in the products, or in other terms, to determine the relative value of labor, that M. Proudhon seeks for a measure of the relative value of commodities. To determine the measure of the relative value of commodities he can think of nothing better than of giving as the equivalent of a certain quantity of labor the sum of the products that it has created, which amounts to supposing that the whole of society consists solely of direct workers receiving for wages their own produce. In the second place, he sets forth as a fact the equality of the days of different workers. To sum up, he seeks the measure of the relative value of commodities in order to discover the equal remuneration of the workers, and he assumes, as an already established fact, equality of wages in order to discover the relative value of commodities. What admirable dialectic!

" Say and the economists who have followed him have observed that labor being itself subject to valuation, a commodity like any other, in fact, to take it for a principle and the efficient cause of value would be to move in a vicious circle. These economists, if they will permit me to say so, have shown by that a prodigious inattention. Labor is called *value,* not as being a commodity itself, but in view of the values supposed to be potentially embodied in it. The value of labor is a figurative expression, an anticipation of the cause and the effect. It is a fiction of the same kind as the *productivity of capital.* Labor produces, capital denotes value.... Labor, like liberty, is a vague and indefinite

A SCIENTIFIC DISCOVERY

thing by nature, but it becomes qualitatively defined by its object; that is to say, it becomes a reality by its product.

"But what need to insist? When the economist (read M. Proudhon) changes the name of things, *vera rerum vocabula,* he implicitly avows his impotence and puts himself out of court." (Proudhon I., 188.)

We have seen that M. Proudhon makes of the value of labor "the efficient cause" of the value of products to the extent that for him *wages,* the official name of the "value of labor," form the integral price of everything. That is why the objection of Say troubles him. In labor commodity, which is a frightful reality, he sees nothing but a grammatical ellipsis. The whole of existing society, then, based upon labor commodity, is henceforth based upon a poetic licence, on a figurative expression.

Does society desire to "eliminate all the inconveniences" which trouble it, it has only to eliminate all the ill-sounding terms. Let it change the language, and for that it has only to address itself to the Academy and ask it for a new edition of its dictionary. After all that we have seen, it is easy to understand why M. Proudhon, in a work on political economy, has had to enter into long dissertations on etymology and other parts of grammar. Thus, he has still to gravely discuss *servus a servare.* These philological dissertations have a profound meaning, an esoteric meaning; they form an essential part of the argument of M. Proudhon.

Labor, labor force, inasmuch as it is bought and sold, is a commodity the same as any other commodity, and has consequently an exchange-value. But the value of labor, or labor, as a commodity, does not produce, any more than the value of wheat, or wheat, as a commodity, serves for nourishment.

THE POVERTY OF PHILOSOPHY

Labor "is worth" more or less, according as alimentary commodities are more or less dear, according as the supply and demand of "hands" exists in such or such a degree, &c., &c.

Labor is not a "vague thing"; it is always definitely determined labor, never labor in general, which is bought and sold. It is not only the labor which is qualitatively defined by the object, but it is also the object which is determined by the specific quality of the labor.

Labor, in so far as it is bought and sold, is itself a commodity. Why is it purchased? "In view of the values supposed to be potentially embodied in it." But if we say that a certain thing is a commodity there is no question of the object for which we buy it, it is simply for the service we intend to derive from it; the application which we shall make of it. It is a commodity as object of traffic. All the reasonings of M. Proudhon confine themselves to this: We do not purchase labor as an object of immediate consumption. No, we buy it as an instrument of production, as we would buy a machine. Merely as a commodity labor is worth nothing and produces nothing. M. Proudhon might just as well have said that there are no commodities in existence at all, seeing that every commodity is only acquired for some use and never merely as a commodity.

In measuring the value of commodities by labor M. Proudhon vaguely perceives the impossibility of expressing labor by this same measure, in so far as it has a value, labor commodity. He has a misgiving that it is to make of the minimum wage the natural and normal price of direct labor, that it is to accept the existing state of society. So, to escape from this fatal consequence he performs a *volte-face* and pretends that labor is not a commodity, that it could not have a value. He forgets

A SCIENTIFIC DISCOVERY

that he has himself taken labor value for a measure. He forgets that his whole system rests on the labor commodity, on labor which is trafficked, bought and sold, exchanged for products, &c.; on the labor, in fine, which is an immediate source of revenue for the worker. He forgets all.

In order to save his system he consents to sacrifice its basis.

Et propter vitam vivendi perdere causas!

We now arrive at a new definition of "constituted value."

"Value is the *relation of the proportion* of the products which compose wealth."

First of all let us remark that the simple expression "relative or exchangeable value" implies the idea of some sort of relation, in which the products exchange reciprocally. By giving to this relation the name of "relation of proportion" we change nothing of the relative value, except the expression. Neither the depreciation nor the enhancement of the value of a product destroys the quality which it possesses of finding itself in a "relation of proportion" of some kind with the other products which form wealth.

Why, then, this new term, which conveys no new idea?

The "relation of proportion" makes one think of many other economic relations, such as the proportion of production, the just proportion between supply and demand, &c.; and M. Proudhon has thought of all that in formulating this didactic paraphrase of saleable values.

In the first place, the relative value of products being determined by the comparative quantity of labor employed in the production of each of them, the relation

THE POVERTY OF PHILOSOPHY

of the proportion, applied to this special use, signifies the respective quota of products which can be manufactured in a given time, and which, consequently, would be given in exchange.

Let us see what advantage M. Proudhon draws from this relation of proportion. Everybody knows that when supply and demand are equal the relative value of any product whatever is exactly determined by the quantity of labor embodied in it—that is to say, that this relative value expresses the relation of the proportion precisely in the sense in which we have just given it. M. Proudhon reverses the order of things. Begin, says he, by measuring the relative value of a product by the quantity of labor embodied in it, and then supply and demand will infallibly equalise themselves. Production will correspond with consumption; the product will be always exchangeable. Its current price will express precisely its exact value. Instead of saying, with everybody else, that when the weather is fine one sees many people out walking, M. Proudhon makes his people walk out in order to ensure fine weather.

What M. Proudhon gives as the consequence of saleable value determined *à priori* by labor time could only be justified by a law formulated in almost these terms:

Products will henceforth be exchanged in exact ratio to the labor time they have cost. Whatever may be the proportion between supply and demand, the exchange of commodities will be always as if they had been produced proportionately to the demand.

Let M. Proudhon take it on himself to formulate and to make such a law, and we will pass the proofs to him. If he intends on the contrary to justify his theory, not as legislator, but as economist, he will have to prove that the *time* which is necessary to create a commodity in-

A SCIENTIFIC DISCOVERY

dicates exactly its degree of *utility,* and marks its relation of proportion to the demand and, by consequence, to the total mass of wealth. In this case, if a product is sold at a price equal to its cost of production, supply and demand always equalise themselves; since the cost of production is deemed to express the true relation of supply and demand.

Practically M. Proudhon sets himself to prove that the labor-time necessary to create a product marks its exact proportion to existing wants, in such sort that the things of which the production costs the least time are those things which are the most immediately useful, and so on, gradually. The production of an article of luxury in itself proves, according to this doctrine, that society has sufficient leisure to permit it to satisfy a desire for luxury.

The very proof of his thesis M. Proudhon finds in the observation that the things the most useful cost the least time to produce, that society commences always by the most simple industries, and that it successively "attacks the production of objects which cost more labor time, and which correspond to wants of a higher order."

M. Proudhon borrows from M. Dunoyer the example of extractive industry—gathering wild fruit, pasturage, the chase, fishing, &c.—which represents the most simple form of industry, the least costly, and by which man commenced "the first day of his second creation." The first day of his first creation is enshrined in Genesis, which shows us God as the first industrial of the world.

Things go quite otherwise than as M. Proudhon thinks. From the very moment in which civilisation begins production commences to be based on the antagonism of orders, of States, of classes, and finally on the antagonism between accumulated labor and present labor. No antagonism, no progress. That is the law which civilisation has followed down to our day. Up to the present the productive forces have been developed thanks to this *régime* of the antagonism of classes. To say now that, because all the wants of all the workers were satisfied, men could give themselves up to the creation of products of a superior order, more complicated industries, would be to make abstraction of the antagonism of classes, and to overthrow the whole development of history. It is as if one should say that because, under the Roman emperors, murenas were nourished in artificial fishponds, there was food in abundance for all the population of Rome. But, on the contrary, the Roman people wanted the necessary means to buy bread while the Roman aristocrats had no lack of slaves with which to feed their fishes.

The price of food has almost continually risen, while the price of manufactured articles and luxuries has almost continually fallen. Take the agricultural industry itself: the most indispensable objects, such as wheat, meat, &c., increase in price while cotton, sugar, coffee, &c., fall continually in a surprising fashion. Even among food-stuffs, properly so-called, luxuries, such as artichokes, asparagus, &c., are relatively cheaper to-day than the objects of prime necessity. In our epoch the superfluity is more easily produced than the necessaries of life. Finally, at different historical epochs, the reciprocal relations of price are not only different but opposed. All through the Middle Ages agricultural products were relatively cheaper than manufactured products: in modern times the relations are reversed.

A SCIENTIFIC DISCOVERY

Has the utility of agricultural products therefore diminished since the Middle Ages?

The use of products is determined by the social conditions in which the consumers are placed, and these conditions themselves rest on the antagonism of classes.

Cotton, potatoes and spirits are the objects of commonest use. Potatoes have engendered scrofula; cotton has largely driven linen and wool out of the market, although wool and linen are in many cases of much greater utility, if only from considerations of hygiene; spirits, again, have largely replaced beer and wine, although spirits, used as food, are generally recognised to be poison. For a whole century Governments vainly struggled against European opinion; economics prevailed, they dictated orders to consumption.

Why, then, are cotton, potatoes and spirits the pivots of bourgeois society? Because the least amount of labor is necessary for their production, and they are in consequence at the lowest price. Why does the minimum of price decide the maximum of consumption? Can it by any chance be because of the absolute utility of these objects, of their intrinsic utility, of their utility in so far as they correspond in the most useful manner to the needs of the worker, as man, and not of the man as worker? No, it is because, in a society based upon *poverty,* the *poorest* products have the fatal prerogative of serving the use of the greatest number.

To say now that, because the least costly things are most generally used therefore they must be of the greatest utility, is to say that the extensive use of spirits because of their low cost of production is the most conclusive proof of their utility; it is to tell the proletariat that the potato is the most salutary meat; it is to accept the existing state of things; it is, in fine, to make, with M.

THE POVERTY OF PHILOSOPHY

Proudhon, the apology for a society without comprehending it.

In a future society, where the antagonism of classes will have ceased, where there will no longer be classes, use will no longer be determined by the *minimum* time of production; but the time of social production which will be devoted to the various objects will be determined by their degree of social utility.

To return to the thesis of M. Proudhon: From the moment that the labor time necessary to the production of an object is not the expression of its degree of utility, the exchange-value of this object, determined beforehand by the labor time embodied in it, can never regulate the just relation of supply and demand, that is to say, the relation of the proportion in the sense which M. Proudhon for the moment attaches to it.

It is not the sale of any product whatever at the price of its cost of production which constitutes "the relation of proportion" of supply and demand, or the proportional quota of this product relatively to the whole of production; it is the *variations of demand and of supply* which fix for the producer the quantity in which it is necessary to produce a given product in order to get in exchange at least the cost of production. And as these variations are continued, there is also a continual movement of withdrawal and of application of capitals with regard to the different branches of industry.

"It is only by reason of similar variations that capitals are devoted precisely in the required *proportion,* and not beyond, to the production of the different commodities for which there is a demand. By the rise or fall of prices profits rise above or fall below their mean level, and by that capital is attracted to or repelled from the

A SCIENTIFIC DISCOVERY

particular employment which experiences the one or the other of these variations."

"If we cast our eyes over the markets of large towns we shall see with what regularity they are provided with all kinds of commodities, native and foreign, in the required quantity; and whatever difference there may be in demand as the effect of caprice, of taste, or by the variation of population; without there often being a glut by too abundant a supply, or excessive dearness through the poorness of supply compared to demand; we must admit that the principle which distributes capital in each branch of industry in the *exact proportions required,* is more powerful than is generally supposed." (Ricardo, vol. I., pp. 105 and 108.)

If M. Proudhon accepts the value of products as determined by labor time, he must equally accept the oscillatory movement which alone makes labor time the measure of value. There is no "relation of proportion" completely constituted, there is only a constituting movement.

We have seen in what sense it is correct to speak of the "proportion" as of a consequence of value determined by labor time. We will see now how this measure by time, called by M. Proudhon "law of proportion," transforms itself into a law of *disproportion*.

Every new invention which permits of the production in one hour of that which hitherto took two hours to produce depreciates all the homogeneous products already on the market. Competition compels the producer to sell the product of two hours as cheaply as the product of one hour. Competition realises the law according to which the relative value of a product is determined by the labor time necessary to produce it. Labor time,

THE POVERTY OF PHILOSOPHY

serving as measure of saleable value, thus becomes the law of continual depreciation of labor. We will say more. There will be depreciation, not only of the commodities put on the market, but also the instruments of production and of the whole manufacture. This fact Ricardo has already noted in saying: "In constantly increasing the facility of production we constantly reduce the value of the things previously produced."

Sismondi goes further. He sees in this "value *constituted*" by labor time the source of all the contradictions of modern commerce and industry. "Mercantile value," he says, "is always fixed, in the last analysis, by the quantity of labor necessary to procure the thing valued: it is not what it has actually cost, but what it will cost henceforth with perhaps perfect means; and this quantity, however difficult it may be to appreciate, is always established with fidelity by competition. . . . It is on this basis that is calculated the demand of the seller and the offer of the purchaser. The first will perhaps affirm that the thing has cost him ten days' labor; but if the other recognises that he may henceforth accomplish it with eight days' labor, if competition carries the demonstration to the two contracting parties, it will be to eight days only that the value will be reduced, and that the market price will be established. The two contracting parties have indeed, it is true, the notion that the thing is useful, that it is desired, that without desire there would be no sale; but the fixation of price has no connection with utility." ("Études," &c., Vol. II., p. 267, Brussels edition.)

It is important to insist upon this point, that what determines value is not the time in which a thing has been produced, but the minimum time in which it is susceptible

A SCIENTIFIC DISCOVERY

of being produced, and this minimum is demonstrated by competition. Suppose for a moment that there is no longer any competition, and therefore, no means of demonstrating the minimum of labor necessary for the production of a commodity, what would be the result? It would suffice to put six hours' labor into the production of a commodity in order to have the right, according to M. Proudhon, to exact in exchange six times as much as he who has devoted only one hour to the production of the same article.

In place of a "relation of proportion" we have a relation of disproportion, if we are at all times willing to remain in these relations, good or evil.

The continual depreciation of labor is only a single side, only a single consequence of the valuation of commodities by labor time. The inflation of prices, overproduction, and many other of the phenomena of industrial anarchy find their interpretation in this mode of valuation.

But labor time serving as means of value, does it at least give rise to the proportional variety in commodities which so charms M. Proudhon?

On the contrary, monopoly in all its dreary monotony, follows in its train and invades the world of commodities, as, in the sight and to the knowledge of everybody, monopoly invades the world of the instruments of production. It appertains only to certain branches of industry to make very rapid progress, as, for instance, the cotton industry. The natural consequence of this progress is that the products manufactured from cotton fall rapidly in price; but in proportion as the prices of cotton fall the price of linen must rise in comparison. What is the result? Linen is replaced by cotton. It is in this way that linen has been nearly driven out of the

THE POVERTY OF PHILOSOPHY

whole of North America. And we have obtained instead of the proportional variety of product, the reign of cotton.

What now remains of this "relation of proportion." Nothing but the vow of an honest man, who would that the commodities should be produced in such proportions that they can be sold at an honest price. In all times the good bourgeois and the philanthropist economists have been pleased to make this innocent vow.

Let us hear old Bois-Guillebert: "The price of commodities," says he, "must always be *proportioned,* there being only this intelligence which can make them live together to constantly give and receive reciprocally (see the continual exchangeability of M. Proudhon) birth to one another..... As wealth, then, is only this constant intercourse between man and man, between metier and metier, it is a fearful blindness to seek for the cause of poverty elsewhere than in the cessation of such commerce brought about by the derangement in the proportion of prices." ("Dissertations sur la Nature des Richesses.")

Listen also to a modern economist.

"A great law which must be applied to production, is the law of proportion, which can alone preserve the continuity of value..... The equivalent must be guaranteed.... All the nations have essayed at different epochs. by means of numerous commercial regulations and restrictions, to realise up to a certain point this law of proportion; but egoism, inherent in the nature of man, has forced him to overthrow all this regulation *régime.* A proportional production is the realisation of the entire truth of the science of social economy." (W. Atkinson, "Principles of Political Economy," London, 1840, pp. 170-195.)

Fuit Troja. This true proportion between supply and demand which again begins to become the object of so

A SCIENTIFIC DISCOVERY

many vows, has long ceased to exist. It has died of old age. It was only possible in the epoch in which the means of production were limited, and in which exchange only took place within very narrow limits. With the birth of the great industry this just proportion disappeared, and production was fatally constrained to pass in a perpetual succession, through the vicissitudes of prosperity, depression, crisis, stagnation, new prosperity, and so on in succession.

Those who, like Sismondi, would return to the just proportion of production, while conserving the existing bases of society, are reactionary, since, to be consistent, they must also desire to re-establish all the other conditions of past times.

What was it which maintained production in just proportion, or nearly so? It was the demand which governed the supply which preceded it. Production followed consumption step by step. The great industry, forced by the very instruments of which it disposed to produce on an ever-increasing scale, could not wait for the demand. Production preceded consumption, the supply forced the demand.

In existing society, in the industry based on individual exchanges, the anarchy of production, which is the source of so much misery, is at the same time the source of all progress.

Thus of two things, one:

Either you would have the just proportions of past centuries, with the means of production of our epoch, in which case you are at once a reactionary and a utopian;

Or, you would have progress without anarchy: In which case, in order to conserve productive forces, you must abandon individual exchanges.

Individual exchanges accord only with the small

THE POVERTY OF PHILOSOPHY

industry of past centuries and its corollary of " just proportion," or with the great industry and all its train of misery and anarchy.

After all, the determination of value by labor time, that is to say the formula which M. Proudhon has given us as the regenerating formula of the future, is then only the scientific expression of the economic relations of existing society, as Ricardo has clearly and definitely demonstrated it long before M. Proudhon.

But at least the *" equalitarian "* application of this formula belongs to M. Proudhon. Is it he who has first thought of reforming society by transforming all men into immediate workers, exchanging quantities of equal labor? Is it indeed for him to make to the Communists — these people innocent of all knowledge of political economy, these " obstinately stupid men," these " paradisical dreamers "— the reproach of not having found before him, this " solution of the problem of the proletariat "?

Whoever is, no matter how little, acquainted with the movement of political economy in England, knows that nearly all the Socialists of that country have, at different times, proposed the equalitarian application of the Ricardian theory. We may cite to M. Proudhon the " Political Economy " of Hopkins; William Thompson: " An Inquiry into the Principles of the Distribution of Wealth most Conducive to Human Happiness," 1827; T. R. Edmonds: " Practical, Moral, and Political Economy," 1828, &c., &c., and we might add pages of &c. We will content ourselves with quoting an English Communist. We will reproduce the decisive passage of his remarkable work, " Labor's Wrongs and Labor's Remedy," Leeds, 1839, and we will dwell upon it at sufficient length; in the first place, because J. F. Bray is yet but

A SCIENTIFIC DISCOVERY

little known in France; and, further, because we believe we have there found the key of the past, present and future works of M. Proudhon.

"The only way to arrive at truth is to go at once to first principles. . . . Let us go at once to the source from whence governments themselves have arisen. . . . By thus going to the origin of the thing we shall find that every form of government, and every social and governmental wrong, owes its rise to the existing social system — to the institution of property as it at present exists — and that, therefore, if we would end our wrongs and our miseries at once and for ever, the present arrangements of society must be totally subverted, and supplanted by those more in accordance with the principles of justice and the rationality of man.

"By thus fighting them upon their own ground, and with their own weapons, we shall avoid that senseless clatter respecting ' visionaries ' and ' theorists ' with which they are so ready to assail all who dare move one step from that beaten track which ' by authority ' has been pronounced to be the only right one. Before the conclusions arrived at by such a course of proceeding can be overthrown the economists must unsay or disprove those established truths and principles on which their own arguments are founded." (J. F. Bray, pp. 17 and 41.)

"It is labor alone which bestows value. . . . Every man has an undoubted right to all that his honest labor can procure him. When he thus appropriates the fruits of his labor he commits no injustice upon any other human being, for he interferes with no other man's right of doing the same with the produce of his labor. . . . All these ideas of superior and inferior — of master and man — may be traced to the neglect of first principles, and to the consequent rise of inequality of possessions;

THE POVERTY OF PHILOSOPHY

and such ideas will never be eradicated, nor the institutions founded upon them be subverted, so long as this inequality is maintained. Men have hitherto blindly hoped to remedy the present unnatural state of things, and to institute equality of rights and laws by removing one rich tyrant and setting up another—by destroying existing inequality and leaving untouched the cause of the inequality; but it will shortly be seen that it is not in the nature of any mere governmental change to afford permanent relief—that misgovernment is not a cause but a consequence—that it is not the creator, but the created—that it is the offspring of inequality of possessions; and that inequality of possessions is inseparably connected with our present social system." (J. F. Bray, pp. 33, 36 and 37.)

"Not only are the greatest advantages, but strict justice also, on the side of a system of equality..... Every man is a link, and an indispensable link, in the chain of effects—the beginning of which is but an idea, and the end, perhaps, the production of a piece of cloth. Thus, although we may entertain different feelings towards the several parties, it does not follow that one should be better paid for his labor than another. The inventor will ever receive, in addition to his just pecuniary reward, that which genius only can obtain from us—the tribute of our admiration."

"From the very nature of labor and exchange, strict justice not only requires that all exchangers should be mutually, but that they should likewise be equally benefited. Men have only two things which they can exchange with each other, namely, labor, and the produce of labor; therefore, let them exchange as they will, they merely give, as it were, labor for labor. If a just system of exchanges were acted upon, the value

A SCIENTIFIC DISCOVERY

of all articles would be determined by the *entire cost of production, and equal values should always exchange for equal values.* If, for instance, it takes a hatter one day to make a hat, and a shoemaker the same time to make a pair of shoes—supposing the material used by each to be of the same value—and they exchange these articles with each other, they are not only mutually but equally benefited: the advantage derived by either party cannot be a disadvantage to the other, as each has given the same amount of labor, and the materials made use of by each were of equal value. But if the hatter should obtain two pair of shoes for one hat—time and value of material being as before—the exchange would clearly be an unjust one. The hatter would defraud the shoemaker of one day's labor; and were the former to act thus in all his exchanges he would receive for the labor of half a year, the product of some other person's whole year; therefore the gain of the first would necessarily be a loss to the last. We have heretofore acted upon no other than this most unjust system of exchanges—the workmen have given the capitalist the labor of a whole year in exchange for the value of only half a year—and from this, and not from the assumed inequality of bodily and mental powers, in individuals, has arisen the inequality of wealth and power which at present exists around us. It is an inevitable condition of inequality of exchanges—of buying at one price and selling at another —that capitalists shall continue to be capitalists and working men be working men, the one a class of tyrants and the other a class of slaves..... The whole transaction, therefore, plainly shows that the capitalists and proprietors do no more than give the working man, for his labor of one week, a part of the wealth which they obtained from him the week before!—which just amounts

THE POVERTY OF PHILOSOPHY

to giving him *nothing* for *something*. . . . The whole transaction, therefore, between the producer and the capitalist is a palpable deception, a mere farce; it is, in fact, in thousands of instances, no more than a barefaced though a legalised robbery." (J. F. Bray, pp. 45, 48, 49 and 50.)

"The gain of the employer will never cease to be the loss of the employed, until the exchanges between the parties are equal; and exchanges never can be equal while society is divided into capitalists and producers — the last living upon their labor, and the first bloating upon the profit of that labor."

"It is plain," continues Bray, "that you may establish whatever form of government you will . . . that you may talk of morality and brotherly love . . . no such reciprocity can exist where there are unequal exchanges, and inequality of rewards for equal services. . . . Inequality of exchanges, as being the cause of inequality of possessions, is the secret enemy that devours us."

"It has been deduced, also, from a consideration of the intention and end of society, not only that all men should labor, and thereby become exchangers, but that equal values should always exchange for equal values — and that as the gain of one man ought never to be the loss of another, value should ever be determined by cost of production. But we have seen that, under the present arrangements of society, all men do not labor . . . that the gain of the capitalist and the rich man is always the loss of the workman — that this result will invariably take place, and the poor man be left entirely at the mercy of the rich man, so long as there is inequality of exchanges — and that equality of exchanges can be insured only under social arrangements in which labor is universal. . . . If exchanges were equal, the wealth of the present capitalists would gradually go from them to the working classes." (Bray, pp. 51, 52, 53 and 55.)

"So long as the system of unequal exchanges is tolerated, the producers will be almost as poor and as ignorant and as hardworked as they are at present, *even if every Governmental burden be swept away and all taxes be abolished.* . . . Nothing but a total change of system — an equalising of labor and exchanges — can alter this state of things for the better, and ensure men a true equality of rights. . . . The producers have but to make an effort — and by them must every effort for their own redemption be made — and their chains will be snapped asunder for ever. . . . As an end political equality is a failure. As a means, also, it is a failure. . . . Where things are of equal value, and they are exchanged unequally, the gain of one exchanger must ever be the loss of another . . . for every exchange is then simply a transfer, and not a sacrifice of labor and wealth. Thus, although under a social system based on equal exchanges, a parsimonious man may become rich, his wealth will be no more than the accumulated produce of his own labor. He may exchange his wealth or he may give it to others who will exchange it for an equal value of the wealth of other persons; but a rich man cannot continue wealthy for any length of time after he has ceased to labor. Under equality of exchanges, wealth cannot have, as it has now, a procreative and apparently self-generating power, such as replenishes all waste from consumption; for, unless it be renewed by labor, wealth, when once consumed, is given up for ever. That which is now called profit and interest cannot exist, as such, in connection with equality of exchanges, for producer and distributor would be alike remunerated, and the sum total of their labor would determine the value of the article created and brought to

THE POVERTY OF PHILOSOPHY

the hands of the consumer. The principle of equal exchanges, therefore, must, from its very nature, *ensure universal labor.*" (Bray, pp. 67, 88, 89, 94, 109 and 110.) After having rebutted the objections of the economists to communism, Bray continues thus: "If a changed character be essential to the success of the social system of community in its most perfect form—and if, likewise, the present system affords no circumstances and no facilities for effecting the requisite change of character and preparing man for the higher and better state desired, it is evident that things must remain as they are... unless some preparatory steps be discovered and made use of—some movement partaking partly of the present and partly of the desired system, some intermediate resting-place, to which society may go with all its faults and all its follies, and from which it may move forward, imbued with those qualities and attributes without which the system of community and equality cannot as such have existence." (Bray, p. 134.)

"The whole movement would require only co-operation in its simplest form...... Cost of production would in every instance determine value; and equal values would always exchange for equal values. If one person worked a whole week, and another worked only half a week, the first would receive double the remuneration of the last; but this extra pay of the one would not be at the expense of the other, nor would the loss incurred by the last man fall in any way upon the first. Each person would exchange the wages he individually received for commodities of the same value as his respective wages; and in no case could the gain of one man or one trade be a loss to another man or another trade. The labor of every individual would *alone determine* his gain and his losses."

A SCIENTIFIC DISCOVERY

"By means of general and local boards of trade, and the directors attached to each individual company, the quantities of the various commodities required for consumption (the relative value of each in regard to each other), the number of hands required in various trades and descriptions of labor, and all other matters connected with production and distribution, could in a short time be as easily determined for a nation as for an individual company under the present arrangements.... As individuals compose families, and families towns, under the existing system, so likewise would they after the joint-stock change had been effected. The present distribution of people in towns and villages, bad as it is, would not be directly interfered with..... Under this joint-stock system.... every individual would be at liberty to accumulate as much as he pleased, and to enjoy such accumulations when and where he might think proper..... Society would be, as it were, one great joint-stock company, composed of an indefinite number of smaller companies, all laboring, producing and exchanging with each other on terms of the most perfect equality....."

"Our new system of society by shares, which is only a concession made to existing society, in order to arrive at communism, established in such a way as to admit *of individual property in productions in connection with a common property in production powers*—making every individual dependent on his own exertions, and at the same time allowing him an equal participation in every advantage afforded by nature and art—is fitted to take society as it is, and to prepare the way for other and better changes." (Bray, pp. 158, 160, 162, 163, 168, 170 and 194.)

We have only a few words to say in reply to Mr.

THE POVERTY OF PHILOSOPHY

Bray, who, quite in spite of ourselves, we find to have supplanted M. Proudhon, inasmuch as Mr. Bray, far from wishing to have the last word of humanity, only proposes such measures as he believes good for a period of transition between existing society and a system of communism.

An hour of the labor of Peter is exchanged for an hour of the labor of Paul. That is the fundamental axiom of Mr. Bray. Suppose Peter has performed twelve hours' work and Paul has only done six; then Peter will only be able to make with Paul an exchange of six against six. Peter will consequently have six hours' labor remaining. What will he do with these six hours of labor?

Either he will do nothing with them, that is to say he will have worked six hours for nothing; or maybe he will idle six hours in order to equalise matters; or, again, and this is his last resource, he will give to Paul these six hours, with which he can do nothing else, into the bargain.

Thus at the end of the account, what has Peter gained on Paul? Some hours of labor? No. He will have gained only some hours of leisure; he will be compelled to be an idler for six hours. And for this new right of idleness to be not only accepted but appreciated in the new society it is necessary that the latter should find its highest felicity in laziness and that labor should weigh upon it like a chain from which it must free itself at any cost. Yet still, if these hours of leisure which Peter has gained over Paul were only a real gain! But no. Paul, in beginning by working only six hours, arrives by steady and regular labor at the same result as Peter only obtains by commencing with an excess of labor. Each would desire to be Paul, there would be competition

A SCIENTIFIC DISCOVERY

to obtain the position of Paul, a competition in idleness.

Ah well! What has the exchange of equal quantities of labor given us? Overproduction, depreciation, overwork followed by enforced idleness; in fine, the economic relations such as we see them in existing society, less the competition of labor.

But no, we deceive ourselves. There would be still an expedient by which the new society, the society of Peters and Pauls, could be saved. Peter might eat all alone the product of the six hours of labor which remained to him. But from the moment in which there is no more exchanging in order to have a product, there is no longer production in order to exchange, and all the supposition of a society founded on exchange and the division of labor falls to the ground. We should have saved the equality of exchanges, only through the cessation of exchange: Paul and Peter would have arrived at the condition of Robinson Crusoe.

Then if we imagine all the members of society to be workers, the exchange of equal quantities of hours of labor is only possible on condition that we understand beforehand the number of hours necessary to employ in material production. But such an understanding denies individual exchange.

We shall still arrive at the same result if we take for a starting point, not the distribution of the products created, but the act of production. In the great industry Peter is not free to fix for himself the time of his labor, because the labor of Peter is nothing without the co-operation of all the Peters and all the Pauls in the establishment. It is this which clearly explains the obstinate resistance of the English manufacturer to the Ten Hours Bill. They knew very well that a reduction of two hours' labor given to the women and children

THE POVERTY OF PHILOSOPHY

would be sure to result in a reduction of the hours of labor of adult men. It is in the nature of the great industry that the hours of labor should be equal for all. That which is to-day the result of capital and the competition of the workers among themselves, will be to-morrow, if you cut off the relation between labor and capital, the effect of an understanding based on the relation of the sum of the productive forces to the sum of existing wants.

But such an understanding is the condemnation of individual exchange, and so we arrive once more at our first result.

In principle there is no exchange of products, but exchange of the labors which co-operate in production. The mode of exchange of the products depends upon the mode of production of the productive forces. Generally the form of the exchange of products corresponds to the form of production. Change the latter and the former finds itself changed as a consequence. We may also see in the history of society the mode of exchanging products regulated by the method of producing them. Individual exchange also corresponds to a determined method of production, which itself corresponds to the antagonism of classes. Thus there is no individual exchange without the antagonism of classes.

But the honest consciences refuse to accept this evidence. So long as one is bourgeois one cannot do other than see in this relation of antagonism a relation of harmony and eternal justice, which permits no one to get value at the expense of another. For the bourgeois individual exchange can exist without the antagonism of classes; for him these are two entirely incompatible things. Individual exchange, as it presents itself to the

A SCIENTIFIC DISCOVERY

bourgeois, is far from resembling individual exchange as it is in actual practice.

Mr. Bray makes of the *illusion* of the honest bourgeois the *ideal* which he desires to realise. In purifying individual exchange, in freeing it from all the antagonistic elements he finds in it, he believes he has found an *"equalitarian"* relation which he desires to see adopted by society.

Mr. Bray does not see that this equalitarian relation, this *corrective ideal,* which he wishes to apply to the world is itself nothing but the reflection of the existing world, and that it is in consequence quite impossible to reconstitute society on a basis which is only an embellished shadow. In proportion as this shadow becomes substance, it is seen that this substance, far from being the dreamed-of transfiguration, is nothing but the body of existing society.*

SECTION III.—APPLICATION OF THE LAW OF THE PROPORTION OF VALUE.

(A)—Money.

"Gold and silver are the first commodities the value of which has arrived at its constitution."

Gold and silver then are the first applications of the "constituted value" of M. Proudhon. And as M. Proudhon constitutes the values of products in deter-

---

* Like all other theories, this of Mr. Bray has had its partisans who have been deceived by appearances. In London, Sheffield, Leeds, and many other towns in England, have been founded some "equitable-labor-exchange-bazaars." These bazaars, after having absorbed considerable capital, have all failed miserably. People have lost the taste for them for ever. Let M. Proudhon take note!

THE POVERTY OF PHILOSOPHY

mining them by the comparative quantity of labor they embody, all that he had to do was to prove that *variations* which have taken place in the value of gold and silver were always to be explained by the variations in the time of labor necessary to produce them. M. Proudhon does not dream of that. He does not speak of gold and silver as commodities, he speaks of them as money.

All his logic, if logic there be, consists in juggling with the quality which gold and silver possess, of serving as money, for the benefit of all the commodities which have the quality of being valued by labor time. Decidedly there is more of simplicity than malice in this shuffling.

A useful product, being valued by the labor time necessary to produce it, is always acceptable in exchange. Witness, cries M. Proudhon, gold and silver which find themselves in my desired conditions of "exchangeability." Then gold and silver are value arrived at the state of constitution — they are the incorporation of the idea of M. Proudhon. He is most happy in his choice of an example. Gold and silver, in addition to the quality which they possess of being commodities, valued like all other commodities by labor time, have further that of being the universal agent of exchange, of being money. In taking now gold and silver as an application of "value constituted" by labor time, nothing is more easy than to prove that every commodity the value of which may be constituted by labor time will be always exchangeable, will be money.

A very simple question presents itself to the mind of M. Proudhon. Why have gold and silver the privilege of being the type of "constituted value"?

"The particular function which usage has devolved upon the precious metals of serving as the agent of com-

A SCIENTIFIC DISCOVERY

merce is purely conventional, and every other commodity could, less conveniently perhaps, but in a sufficiently satisfactory manner, fill this rôle; the economists recognise and cite more than one example of this. What, then, is the reason for this preference generally accorded to the precious metals, of serving as money, and how is this specialty of functions of money, without analogy in political economy, to be explained. . . . Is it possible to re-establish the series from which money seems to have been detached, and thereby to bring it back to its true principle?"

Already, in putting the question in these terms, M. Proudhon has supposed the existence of money. The first question he should have put is, why, in the exchanges, as they are actually constituted, exchange-value should have had to be individualised, so to speak, by the creation of a special agent of exchange? Money is not a thing, it is a social relation. Why is the relation of money a relation of production, like every other economic relation, such as the division of labor, &c.? If M. Proudhon had clearly ascertained this relation he would not have seen in money an exception, a member detached from a series, unknown or to be discovered.

He would, on the contrary, have recognized that this relation is a link of, and as such, intimately attached to, the whole chain of the other economic relations, and that this relation corresponds to a determined mode of production, neither more nor less than individual exchange. What does he do? He begins by detaching money from the whole of the existing mode of production, in order later to make it the first member of an imaginary series, a series to be discovered.

Once the necessity for a special agent of exchange, that is to say the necessity for money, is recognised, it is

THE POVERTY OF PHILOSOPHY

only necessary to explain why this particular function has devolved upon gold and silver rather than upon any other commodity. That is a secondary question which is not explained by the chain of the relations of production, but by the specific qualities inherent in gold and silver as material. If, after all, the economists on this occasion have "gone outside their own science and have made this a physical, a mechanical, and historical question, &c.," as M. Proudhon has reproached them with having done, they have only done what they ought. The question is no longer within the domain of political economy.

"What none of the economists," says M. Proudhon, "has either seen or comprehended, is the *economic reason* which has determined, in favor of the precious metals, the privilege which they enjoy."

The economic reason which no one, and with good cause, has either seen or comprehended, M. Proudhon has seen, comprehended, and bequeathed to posterity.

"But what no one has remarked is that, of all commodities, gold and silver are the first the value of which has been constituted. In the patriarchal period, gold and silver were bought and sold and exchanged in ingots, but even then with an obvious tendency to domination, and with a marked preference. Little by little monarchs took possession of them and set their seal upon them; and from this sovereign consecration sprang money, that is to say the commodity *par excellence,* which in spite of all the shocks of commerce, maintains a fixed proportioned value and makes itself accepted in payment everywhere..... The distinctive feature of gold and silver, I repeat, arise from this that, thanks to their metallic properties, to the difficulties attending their production, and, above all, to the intervention of the public authority, they have at an early stage, conquered, as commodities, fixity and authenticity."

To say that, of all commodities, gold and silver are the first the value of which has been constituted, is to say, after all which has preceded it, that gold and silver are the first commodities which have become money. That is the great revelation of M. Proudhon, that is the truth which no one had discovered before him!

If by these words M. Proudhon has wished to say that gold and silver are commodities the time necessary to the production of which has been sooner known than in the case of any others, that would still be one of the suppositions with which he is so ready to gratify his readers. If we wished to hold to this patriachal erudition, we should say to M. Proudhon that the time necessary for the production of the objects of prime necessity, such as iron, &c., was known in the first place. We would make him a present of the classic arch of Adam Smith.

But, after all, how can M. Proudhon speak of the constitution of a value, since one value is never constituted alone? It is constituted not by the time which is necessary for its production alone, but relatively to the quota of all other products which can be created in the same time. Thus the constitution of the value of gold and silver presupposes the constitution to be already established of a mass of other products.

It is then, not the commodity which has arrived, in gold and silver, at the state of "constituted value," it is the "constituted value" of M. Proudhon which has arrived, in gold and silver, at the state of money.

Let us now examine more closely these *economic reasons*, which, according to M. Proudhon, have afforded gold and silver the advantage of being erected into money

THE POVERTY OF PHILOSOPHY

sooner than all other products, of passing to the constitutive state of value.

These economic reasons are: the "marked preference," already in "the patriarchal period," and other circumlocutions of the same fact, which augment the difficulty, since they multiply the fact in multiplying the incidents which M. Proudhon brings forward to explain the fact. M. Proudhon has not yet exhausted all the pretended economic reasons. Here is one of supreme force, irresistible:

"It is from the sovereign consecration that money springs; the monarchs seize gold and silver and place their seal upon them."

Thus the good pleasure of monarchs is, for M. Proudhon, the supreme reason, in political economy!

Truly it is necessary to be entirely innocent of all historical knowledge not to know that in all times sovereigns have had to submit to the economic conditions and have never made laws for these. Legislation, political as well as civil, could do no more than give expression to the will of the economic conditions.

Has the monarch seized gold and silver to make them the universal agents of exchange by impressing his seal upon them, or have these universal agents of exchange not rather taken possession of the monarch by forcing him to impress his seal upon them and thus give them a political consecration?

The imprint which has been, and is, given to money is not that of its value, it is that of its weight. The fixity and authenticity of which M. Proudhon speaks applies only to the standard of the money, and this standard indicates how much of material metal there is in a coined piece of gold or silver. "The sole intrinsic value of a silver mark," said Voltaire, with his usual

A SCIENTIFIC DISCOVERY

good sense, " is that of a mark of silver — a half pound of the weight of eight ounces. The weight and the standard alone make this intrinsic value." (Voltaire, " Système de Law.") But the question: What is the value of an ounce of gold or of silver? still remains. If a cashmere from the establishment of the great Colbert bore the trade mark of the manufactory, *pure wool,* this mark would still not tell us the value of the cashmere. The question of how much the wool was worth would still remain. " Philippe I., King of France," says M. Proudhon, " mixed with the pound (sterling) of Charlemagne a third of alloy, imagining that as he alone had the monopoly of the manufacture of money he could do what any trader having a monopoly can do. What was the effect of this alteration of the coinage with which Philippe and his successors have been so strongly reproached? A very sound reasoning, from the commercial point of view, but very unsound in economic science, is to suppose that, as supply and demand regulate value, it is possible, either by producing an artificial scarcity or by monopolising the manufacture, to increase the estimation and consequently the value of things, and that this is true of gold and silver as well as of corn, wine, oil or tobacco. However, the fraud of Philippe was no sooner suspected than his money was reduced to its proper value, and he at once lost all that he imagined he had gained out of his subjects. The same thing would happen as the result of any similar attempts."

To begin with, it has been demonstrated over and over again that if the monarch debases the coinage it is he who suffers the loss. What he has gained once by the first issue he loses as many times as the falsified money returns to him in the form of duties, taxes, &c. But Philippe and his successors knew how to more or

THE POVERTY OF PHILOSOPHY

less protect themselves from this loss, as, once the debased money was put in circulation, they had nothing to do but to order a general reminting of money at the old standard.

And, besides, if Philippe I. had really reasoned like M. Proudhon, Philippe would not have reasoned well "from the commercial point of view." Neither Philippe I. nor M. Proudhon show any evidence of mercantile genius when they imagine that it is possible to alter the value of gold as well as that of every other commodity, simply because that value is determined by the relation of supply and demand.

If King Philippe had ordered that a quarter of wheat should be henceforth called two quarters he would have been a swindler. He would have deceived all the fund-holders, all the people who had to receive a hundred quarters of wheat; he would have been the cause of all these people receiving, instead of a hundred quarters, only fifty. Suppose the king to owe a hundred quarters of wheat, he would have only really had to pay fifty. But in commerce a hundred such quarters would never be worth more than fifty. In changing the name we do not change the thing. The quantity of wheat, either in supply or demand, would not be diminished or increased by this simple change of name. Thus, the relation of supply to demand being precisely the same in spite of this change of name, the price of the wheat would undergo no real alteration. In speaking of the supply and demand of things we do not speak of the supply and demand of the name of things. Philippe I. was not the maker of gold or silver, as Proudhon says; he was the maker of the name of moneys. Make your French cashmeres pass for Asiatic cashmeres, and it is possible that you may deceive a buyer or two; but once the

A SCIENTIFIC DISCOVERY

fraud becomes known, and your pretended Asiatic cashmeres will fall to the price of the French article. In giving a false standard to gold and silver, King Philippe could only make dupes so long as the fraud was not known. Like any other shopkeeper, he deceived his customers by a false description of the commodity, but that could not last long. Sooner or later he must suffer the rigor of the laws of commerce. Is it that which M. Proudhon wishes to prove? No. According to him it is from the monarch, and not from commerce, that money receives its value. And what is it that he has effectively proved? That commerce is more sovereign than the monarch. Let the monarch order that a mark shall be henceforth two marks, commerce will always tell you that these two marks are only worth one mark as before.

But for all that, the question of the determination of value by the quantity of labor has not been taken a step further. It still remains to be decided if the value of these two marks—again become the original mark—is determined by the cost of production or by supply and demand.

M. Proudhon continues: "It may be equally assumed that if, instead of altering the money it had been in the power of the King to double its quantity, the exchange-value of gold and silver would have immediately fallen to half, always in consequence of this proportion and equilibrium."

If this opinion, which M. Proudhon shares with the economists, is correct, it is a proof in support of their theory of supply and demand, and not in support of the "proportion" of M. Proudhon. Because, whatever may have been the quantity of labor embodied in the double quantity of gold and silver its value would have fallen by

THE POVERTY OF PHILOSOPHY

half, the demand remaining the same and the supply having doubled. Or is it indeed, by chance, that "*the law of proportion*" confounds itself this time with the so-despised law of supply and demand? This just proportion of M. Proudhon is in effect so elastic, it lends itself to so many variations, combinations and permutations, that it may possibly for once coincide with the relation of supply and demand.

To "make every commodity acceptable in exchange, if not in fact at least by right," in basing it on the function performed by gold and silver, is then to misunderstand this function. Gold and silver are only acceptable in exchange by right, because they are so in fact, and they are so in fact because the existing organisation of production has need of a universal agent of exchange. The right is only the official recognition of the fact.

We have seen this, that the example of money as an application of value passed to the state of constitution has been chosen by M. Proudhon only that he might smuggle in the whole of his theory of exchangeability; that is to say, in order to demonstrate that every commodity valued by its cost of production must arrive at the state of money. All that would be beautiful and good but for the difficulty that precisely gold and silver — as money — are of all commodities the only ones which are not determined by their cost of production; and that is so far true that in circulation they may be replaced by paper. Inasmuch as there will be a certain proportion observed between the needs of circulation and the quantity of money issued, whether the money be in paper, in gold, in platinum, or in copper, there can be no question of any proportion to the observed between the intrinsic value (the cost of production) and the nominal value of

A SCIENTIFIC DISCOVERY

money. Undoubtedly, in international commerce the value of money, as that of every other commodity, is determined by labor time. But that is simply because gold and silver in international commerce are means of exchange as products and not as money; that is to say, that in this connection gold and silver lose that very character of "fixity and authenticity," of "sovereingn consecration," which is for M. Proudhon their specific characteristic. Ricardo has so well understood this truth that after having based his whole system on value determined by labor time and after having said, "Gold and silver, as well as all other commodities, have value only in proportion to the quantity of labor necessary to produce them and put them on the market," he added, nevertheless, that the value of money is not determined by the labor time embodied in its substance, but only by the law of supply and demand. "Although paper money has no intrinsic value, nevertheless if its quantity be limited its exchangeable value may equal the value of metallic money of the same denomination, or of bullion estimated as specie. It is by the same principle, that is to say by the limitation of the quantity of money, that coins of a low standard are able to circulate at the same value as they would have had if their weight and their value were those fixed by law, and not at the intrinsic value of the pure metal which they contain. That is why in the history of English money we find that our currency has never been depreciated in the same proportion as it has been changed. The reason is that it has never been multiplied in proportion to its depreciation" (Ricardo.)

J. B. Say, on the subject of this passage of Ricardo, observes:

"This example should suffice, it seems to me, to con-

THE POVERTY OF PHILOSOPHY

vince the author that the basis of all value is not the quantity of labor necessary to produce a commodity, but the need which exists for that commodity, balanced by its scarcity."

Thus money, which is for Ricardo no longer a value determined by labor time and which J. B. Say takes for that reason as an example to convince Ricardo that other values cannot be any more than money, determined by labor time, this money, I say, which is taken by J. B. Say as the example of value determined exclusively by supply and demand, becomes for M. Proudhon the example, par excellence, of the application of value constituted . . . by labor time.

To conclude, if money is not a "value constituted" by labor time, still less can it have anything in common with the "just proportion" of M. Proudhon. Gold and silver are always exchangeable, because they have the particular function of serving as the universal agent of exchange, and not at all because they exist in a proportionate quantity to the mass of wealth; or, to speak more correctly, they are always in proportion because, alone of all commodities, they serve as money, as the universal agent of exchange; whatever may be their quantity relatively to the whole mass of wealth. "The money in circulation can never be sufficient to cause a glut; because if you reduce its value you augment its quantity in the same proportion, and in increasing its value you diminish the quantity." (Ricardo.)

"What an imbroglio is political economy!" cries M. Proudhon.

"Accursed gold!" ironically exclaims a Communist (by the mouth of M. Proudhon). It would be as reasonable to say: Accursed wheat, accursed vines, accursed sheep! seeing that "in the same way as gold and silver,

A SCIENTIFIC DISCOVERY

all commercial value must arrive at its exact and rigorous determination."

The idea of sheep and vines being brought to the state of money is not new. In France that idea belongs to the period of Louis XIV. At that epoch, money having begun to establish its omnipotence, there was great complaint of the depreciation of all other commodities, and the people prayed most ardently for the moment in which " every commercial value " would arrive at its exact and rigorous determination, at the state of money. . . . Here is what we find in Bois-Guillebert, one of the oldest economists of France: " Money then, by this growth of innumerable competitors, which will be the commodities themselves established in their exact values, will be restricted to its natural limits." (" Economistes Financiers du Dixhuitième Siècle," p. 422.)

We see that the first illusions of the bourgeoisie are also their last.

(B.) — *Surplus Labor.*

" We read in some works on political economy this absurd hypothesis: *If the price of all things were doubled.* . . . As if the price of all things was not the proportion of things, and as if one could double a proportion, a relation, a law!" (Proudhon, vol. I., page 81.)

The economists have fallen into this error through not having known how to apply the " law of proportion " and of " constituted value "!

Unfortunately we find in the work of M. Proudhon (Vol. I., p. 110) this absurd hypothesis, that " if wages were raised generally, the price of everything would rise." Furthermore, if the phrase in question is found in a work of political economy, there is also the

THE POVERTY OF PHILOSOPHY

explanation. "If we say that the prices of all commodities rise or fall, we always exclude one commodity or another, the commodity excluded being generally either money or labor." ("Encyclopædia Metropolitaine, or Universal Dictionary of Knowledge," vol. IV., the article on Political Economy by Senior, London. 1836.) See also, on this expression, John Stuart Mill, "Essays on some Unsettled Questions of Political Economy," London, 1844, and Tooke, "A History of Prices, &c.," London, 1838.

Let us now pass to the second application of "constituted value," and other proportionalities, whose single failing is that they are so little proportioned, and see if M. Proudhon is more happy in that than in the monetisation of sheep.

"An axiom generally admitted by the economists is that all labor must leave a surplus. This proposition is for me a universal and absolute truth: it is the corollary of the law of proportion, which may be regarded as the summary of the whole science of economy. But, I must crave the pardon of the economists, the principle that *all labor must leave a surplus* has, in their theory, no meaning, and is not susceptible of demonstration." (Proudhon.)

In order to prove that all labor must leave a surplus, M. Proudhon personifies society; he makes a *personal society*, a society which is not, so much as it is necessary, the society of persons, since it has its laws apart, having nothing in common with the people composing society, and its "own intelligence," which is not the common intelligence of men but an intelligence which has no common sense. M. Proudhon reproaches the economists with not having understood the personality of this collective being. We are pleased to oppose to him the

A SCIENTIFIC DISCOVERY

following passage from an American economist who reproaches the other economists with quite the opposite fault. "The moral entity in the grammatical being called society has been clothed with attributes which have no existence except in the imagination of those who make a thing with a word.... that it is which has led to so many difficulties and to such deplorable mistakes in political economy." (Th. Cooper, "Lectures on the Elements of Political Economy," Columbia, 1826.)

"This principle of the surplus of labor," continues M. Proudhon, "is true of individuals only because it emanates from society, which thus confers upon them the benefit of its own laws."

Does M. Proudhon wish by that to say simply that the production of the social individual exceeds that of the isolated individual? Is it of this surplus of the production of associated individuals over that of non-associated individuals that M. Proudhon is to be understood to speak? If that is so we can cite a hundred economists who have expressed this simple truth without all the mysticism with which M. Proudhon surrounds it. Here is what Sadler, for instance, says on the subject:

"Combined labor gives results which individual labor could never produce. In proportion, then, as people increase in number, the products of their united industry will greatly exceed the sum of a simple addition calculated on this increase..... In mechanical arts, as in the labors of science, a man can actually do more in a day than an isolated individual could do in the whole of his life. The axiom of the mathematician, that the whole is equal to the parts, is not true, as applied to this subject. As to labor, the great pillar of human existence, it may be said that the product of accumulated efforts greatly exceeds all that individual and separate efforts could

THE POVERTY OF PHILOSOPHY

ever accomplish." (T. Sadler, " The Law of Population," London, 1830.)

To return to M. Proudhon. The surplus of labor, he says, explains itself by society personified. The life of this personal society follows laws opposed to the laws by which man acts as an individual, as he will prove by " facts."

" The discovery of an economic process can never be worth to the inventor the profit which it yields to society. . . . It has been remarked that railway undertakings have been much less a source of riches to the owners than to the State. . . . The average price for the transport of commodities by road is eighteen centimes per ton per kilometre, goods called for and delivered. It has been calculated that at this rate, an ordinary railway undertaking would not clear ten per cent. net profit, a return nearly equal to that of road cartage. But, admitting that the speed of railway transport is to road transport as four to one, as in society time is money, the railway would show an advantage over the road of four hundred per cent. This enormous advantage, however, very real for society, is far from being realised in the same proportion by the railway proprietor, who, while he enables society to enjoy an additional value of four hundred per cent., does not draw, himself, even ten per cent. Let us suppose, to make the matter clearer, that the railway increases its tariff to twenty-five centimes, that of road transport remaining at eighteen, it would immediately lose all its consignments. Traders and their consignees, everybody, in fact, would return to the old road waggons. The locomotive would be deserted. A social advantage of four hundred per cent. would be sacrificed to a loss of thirty-five per cent. The reason is easy to comprehend: the advantage arising from

A SCIENTIFIC DISCOVERY

the speed of the railway is entirely social, and each individual participates in it only in a minimum proportion (remember we are dealing here only with the transport of merchandise), while the loss falls directly upon the consumer personally. A social benefit of four hundred represents for the individual, if the society only number a million men, four ten-thousandths; while a loss of thirty-three per cent. for the consumer would suppose a social deficit of thirty-three millions." (Proudhon.)

M. Proudhon not only expresses a quadrupled speed by four hundred per cent. of the primitive celerity, but he sets up a relation between the percentage of speed and the percentage of profit, and establishes a proportion between two conditions which, although they may be separately estimated at so much per cent., are nevertheless incommensurable with each other: This is to establish a proportion between the percentages and to leave out the denominations. Percentages are always percentages. Ten per cent. and four hundred per cent. are commensurable, they are to each other as ten is to four hundred. Then, concludes M. Proudhon, a profit of ten per cent. is worth forty times less than a quadrupled speed. In order to save appearances he says that, for society, time is money. This error arises from the fact that he confusedly recollects that there is a relation between value and labor time, and he has nothing to do but assimilate labor time with the time of transport; that is to say, he identifies the drivers, guards and firemen, whose labor time is nothing but the time of transport, with the whole of society. For this master stroke, behold speed become capital, and in such case he is quite right to say: " A benefit of four hundred per cent. would be sacrificed to a loss of thirty-five per cent."

THE POVERTY OF PHILOSOPHY

After having set up this strange proposition as a matehematician, he gives us the explanation as an economist.

"A social benefit equal to four hundred represents for the individual, if the society is only one of a million of men, four ten-thousandths." Certainly; but it is not a question of four hundred, it is a question of four hundred per cent., and a benefit of four hundred per cent. represents neither more nor less than four hundred per cent. for the individual. Whatever may be the capital, the dividends will be always in the proportion of four hundred per cent. What does M. Proudhon do? He takes the percentage for the capital, and, as though he feared that his confusion was not sufficiently manifest, sufficiently "clear," he continues:—

"A loss of thirty-three per cent. for the consumer would suppose a social deficit of thirty-three millinns." Thirty-three per cent. of loss for the consumer would remain a loss of thirty-three per cent. for a million consumers. How can M. Proudhon say afterwards, definitely, that the social deficit, in the case of a loss of thirty-three per cent., would amount to thirty-three millions when he does not know either the social capital or even that of a single one of those interested? Thus, it is not sufficient for M. Proudhon to have confounded the capital and the percentage, but he must go further still, and identify the *capital* put into an undertaking with the *number* of those concerned. "Let us suppose, to make the matter still clearer," a determined capital. A social profit of four hundred per cent. shared among a million participants, supposing each to be interested to the extent of a franc, would mean four francs profit per head, and not 0.0004, as M. Proudhon pretends. In the same way a loss of thirty-three per cent. for each of the participants would represent a social deficit of 330,000

A SCIENTIFIC DISCOVERY

francs, and not thirty-three millions (100:33=1,000,000: 330,000).

M. Proudhon, preoccupied with his theory of personified society, forgets to make the division by 100. He thus obtains 330,000 francs loss; but four francs per head profit make for the society a profit of four million francs. There remains for society a net profit of 3,670,000 francs. This account exactly demonstrates the opposite to that which M. Proudhon wished to demonstrate, that is, that the profits and losses of society are not in inverse ratio to the profits and losses of the individual.

After having rectified these simple errors of calculation, let us glance for a moment at the consequences to which we should arrive if we were to admit for railways this relation of speed to capital such as M. Proudhon gives it, less the errors of calculation. Suppose a transport four times as rapid cost four times as much, this transport would not give less profit than the road transport which is four times as slow and costs only a quarter as much. Then if the latter charges eighteen centimes the railway could charge seventy-two centimes. This would be, according to "mathematical rigor," the consequence of the supposition of M. Proudhon, always excepting his errors of calculation. But then he suddenly tells us that if, instead of seventy-two centimes the railway charged twenty-five it would at once lose all its consignments. Decidedly it would be necessary to return to the old road waggons. Only if we have any advice to offer M. Proudhon it is not to forget in his "Programme of the Progressive Association" to make the division by 100. But, alas! it is scarcely to be hoped that our advice will be listened to, for M. Proudhon is so enamored of his "progressive" calculation, corresponding to the "progressive occasion" that he cries with

THE POVERTY OF PHILOSOPHY

much emphasis: " I have already shown in Chapter II., by the solution of the contradiction of value, that the advantage of every useful discovery is incomparably less for the inventor, whoever he may be, than for society. I have carried out the demonstration of this point with mathematical rigor!"

Let us return to the fiction of society personified, a fiction which has no other object than to prove the following simple truth: A new invention causing a larger quantity of commodities to be produced with the same amount of labor, results in a fall in the saleable value of the product. Society makes a profit then, not in obtaining more exchangeable values, but in obtaining more commodities for the same value. As to the inventor, competition causes his profit to fall successively to the general level of profits. Has M. Proudhon proved this proposition as well as he wished to do? No. That does not prevent him from reproaching the economists with having failed to make this demonstration. To prove to him the contrary we will only cite Ricardo and Lauderdale; Ricardo, the chief of the school which determines value by labor time, Lauderdale one of the most vigorous defenders of the determination of value by supply and demand. Both have developed the same thesis.

" In constantly augmenting the facility of production, we constantly diminish the value of some of the things already produced, although by the same means we not only add to the national wealth, but we increase the facility of producing for the future. . . . As soon as, by means of machines, or by our knowledge of physics, we force natural agents to do the work which has previously been done by man, the value of this work falls in consequence. If it takes ten men to turn a corn-mill, and it is discovered that by means of wind or water the

A SCIENTIFIC DISCOVERY

labor of these ten men can be saved, the flour which will be the product of the action of the mill will, from that moment, fall in value, in proportion to the amount of labor saved; and society will find itself enriched by all the value of the things which the labor of these ten men can produce, the funds destined to the support of the workers not having by that suffered the least diminution." (Ricardo.)

Lauderdale, in his turn, says:—

" There is no part of the capital of a country that more obviously derives its profits from supplanting a portion of labor that would otherwise be performed by man, or from performing a portion which is beyond the reach of his personal exertion, than that which is vested in machinery. . . . The small profit which the proprietors of machinery generally acquire, when compared with the wages of labor which the machine supplants, may perhaps create a suspicion of the rectitude of this opinion. Some fire-engines, for instance, draw more water from a coalpit in one day than could be conveyed on the shoulders of three hundred men, even assisted by the machinery of buckets; and a fire-engine undoubtedly performs its labor at a much smaller expense than the amount of the wages of those whose labor it thus supplants. This is, in truth, the case with all machinery. All machines must execute the labor that was antecedently performed, at a cheaper rate than it could be done by the hand of man. . . . If such a privilege is given for the invention of a machine, which performs, by the labor of one man a quantity of work that used to take the labor of four; as the possession of the exclusive privilege prevents any competition in doing the work, but what proceeds from the labor of the four workmen, their wages, as long as the patent continues, must obviously

THE POVERTY OF PHILOSOPHY

form the measure of the patentee's charge; that is, to secure employment, he has only to charge a little less than the wages of the labor which the machine supplants. But when the patent expires, other machines of the same nature are brought into competition; and then his charge must be regulated on the same principle as every other, according to the abundance of machines.... The profit of capital employed in foreign trade, though it arises from supplanting labor, comes to be regulated, not by the value of the labor it supplants, but, as in all other cases, by the competition among the proprietors of capital, and it will be great or small in proportion to the quantity of capital that presents itself for performing the duty, and the demand for it." ("An Enquiry into the Nature and Origin of Public Wealth.")

Finally, then, in proportion as the profit may be greater than in other industries, fresh capital will be thrown into the new industry until the average profits in it have fallen to the common level.

We have just seen that the illustration of the railway was scarcely appropriate for throwing any light on the fiction of personified society. Nevertheless, M. Proudhon hardly continues his discourse: "These points cleared, nothing is more easy than to explain how labor must leave to each producer a surplus."

This which now follows belongs to classic antiquity. It is a poetic romance told in order to relieve the reader from the fatigue he has suffered from the rigor of the mathematical demonstrations which have preceded it. M. Proudhon gives to his personified society the name of Prometheus, whose noble traits he glorifies in these terms:

"At first, Prometheus, springing from the bosom of nature, awakes to life in an inertia full of charms, &c.,

A SCIENTIFIC DISCOVERY

&c. Prometheus sets to work, and from his first day, the first day of the second creation, the product of Prometheus, that is to say his wealth, his well-being, is equal to ten. The second day Prometheus divides his labor, and his product becomes equal to a hundred. The third day and every following day, Prometheus invents machines, discovers new utilities in his body, new forces in nature. . . . At each step that his industry takes the amount of his production increases, and denotes to him an increase of felicity. And finally, since, for him, to consume is to produce, it is clear that each day's consumption, absorbing only the product of yesterday, leaves a surplus product for the day after."

This Prometheus of M. Proudhon is a droll sort of fellow, as feeble in logic as in political economy. In so far as Prometheus only informs us of the division of labor, the application of machinery, the exploitation of natural forces and scientific power, multiplying the productive forces of men and giving a surplus as compared with the product of isolated labor, this new Prometheus has only the misfortune of coming too late. But when Prometheus begins to speak of production and consumption he becomes really grotesque. To consume is, for him, to produce; he consumes next day that which he produced the day before—thus he has always a day in hand; this day in hand is his "surplus of labor." But in consuming the next day that which he produced the day before, it is necessary that on the first day, which had no yesterday, he should have worked two days, in order to afterwards have a day in hand. How did Prometheus gain this surplus on the first day, when there was neither division of labor, nor machinery, nor even any knowledge of physical forces except fire? Thus the question, in order to have been deferred to

THE POVERTY OF PHILOSOPHY

"the first day of the second creation," has not advanced a step. This manner of explaining things derived at the same time from the Greek and the Hebrew, which is at once mystic and allegorical, gives to M. Proudhon the perfect right to say, "I have demonstrated by theory and by fact the principle that all labor must leave a surplus."

The facts, they are the famous progressive calculation; the theory, it is the myth of Prometheus.

"But," continues M. Proudhon, "this principle, accurate as an arithmetical proposition, is yet far from being realised for everybody. While by the progress of collective industry, each day of individual labor creates a larger and still larger product, and by a necessary consequence, while the worker, with the same wages, must become richer every day, there exist in society some classes which thrive and others which perish."

In 1770 the population of the United Kingdom of Great Britain was fifteen millions and the productive population three millions. The scientific power of production would about equal a population of twelve more millions; thus making a total of fifteen millions of productive forces. Thus the productive power was to the population as 1 is to 1, and the scientific power was to manual power as 4 is to 1.

In 1840 the population did not exceed thirty millions: the productive population was six millions, while the scientific power amounted to 650 millions, that is to say that it was to the whole population as 21 to 1, and to manual power as 108 to 1.

In English society, the day of labor had thus acquired in seventy years a surplus of 2,700 per cent. of productivity, that is to say that in 1840 it produced twenty-seven times as much as in 1770. According to M. Proudhon it is necessary to put the following question:

A SCIENTIFIC DISCOVERY

Why is the English workman of 1840 not twenty-seven times richer than the workman of 1770? In putting such a question one would naturally suppose that the English had been able to produce these riches without the historical conditions in which they were produced — such as: the private accumulation of capital; the modern division of labor; the automatic workshop; anarchic competition; the wage-system, and, in fine, all that which is based upon the antagonism of classes — having to exist. But these were precisely the necessary conditions for the development of the productive forces and of the surplus of labor. Thus, it was necessary, in order to obtain this development of the productive forces, and this surplus of labor, that there should be some classes which thrive and others which perish.

What then, in the last place, is this Prometheus resuscitated by M. Proudhon? It is society, it is the social relations based on the antagonism of classes. These relations are, not the relations of individual to individual, but of workman to capitalist, of farmer to landlord, &c. Efface these relations and you have extinguished the whole of society, and your Prometheus is nothing more than a phantom without arms or legs, that is to say without the automatic workshop, without the division of labor, wanting, in fine, all that you have originally endowed him with in order to enable him to obtain this surplus of labor.

If then, in theory, it suffices to interpret, as M. Proudhon does, the formula of the surplus of labor in the sense of equality without taking account of the actual conditions of production, it must suffice, in practice, to make among the workers an equal distribution of wealth without changing anything in the actual conditions of

THE POVERTY OF PHILOSOPHY

production. This distribution would not assure a great degree of comfort to each of the participants.

But M. Proudhon is not so pessimistic as one might believe him to be. As proportion is everything for him, it is indeed necessary that he should see in his fully endowed Prometheus, that is to say in actual society, a commencement of the realisation of his favorite idea.

"But everywhere also the progress of riches, that is to say *the proportion of values,* is the dominant law; and when the economists oppose to the complaints of the social party the progressive growth of the public wealth and the amelioration effected in the condition of even the most unfortunate classes, they proclaim, without suspecting it, a truth which is the condemnation of their theories."

What, in effect, are collective riches, public wealth? They are the wealth of the bourgeoisie, and not that of each individual bourgeois. Well! the economist have simply demonstrated how, in the relations of production as they exist, the wealth of the bourgeoisie has developed and must still grow. As to the working classes, it is still a much debated question whether their condition has been ameliorated at all as a result of the growth of the so-called public wealth. If the economists cite to us, in support of their optimism, the example of the workers engaged in the English cotton industry, they only notice their position in the rare moments of commercial prosperity. These moments of prosperity are to the epochs of crisis and stagnation in the "exact proportion" of three to ten. But perhaps also, in speaking of amelioration, the economists may have wished to refer to the millions of workers condemned to perish, in the East Indies, in order to procure for the million and a half of

A SCIENTIFIC DISCOVERY

workpeople employed in England in the same industry, three years of prosperity out of ten.

As to the temporary participation in the growth of public wealth, that is different. The fact of the temporary participation is explained by the theory of the economists. It is the confirmation of that theory and not the "condemnation," as M. Proudhon says. If there was anything to condemn it would certainly be the system of M. Proudhon, which, as we have demonstrated, would reduce the worker to the minimum wage, in spite of the growth of riches. It is only by reducing the worker to the minimum wage that he could make an application of the "exact proportion" of values, of "value constituted"—by labor time. It is because wages, in consequence of competition, oscillate above and below the price of the necessaries of life essential to the sustentation of the worker that he can not only participate, to however small a degree, in the development of the collective wealth, but also that he can perish of want. There is the whole theory of the economists, which sets up no illusions.

After his long divagations on the subject of railways, of Prometheus and of the new society to be reconstituted on "constituted value," M. Proudhon reflects; emotion overcomes him, and in a paternal tone he cries:

"*I adjure* the economists to question themselves a moment, in the silence of their hearts, far from the prejudices which disturb them and without regard to the employments which occupy, or which await them, to the interests which they serve so ill, to the approbation to which they aspire, or to the distinctions which their vanity craves; that they should say if to this day the principle that all labor must leave a surplus has been apparent to them with this chain of preliminaries and of consequences that we have raised."

CHAPTER II.

THE METAPHYSICS OF POLITICAL ECONOMY.

SECTION I.— THE METHOD.

Now we are quite in Germany! We have now to talk metaphysics while speaking of political economy. And, in this again, we only follow the " contradictions " of M. Proudhon. Just now he compelled us to speak English, to become even passably English ourselves. Now the scene changes. M. Proudhon transports us to our dear native land and compels us in spite of ourselves to once more assume our quality of German.

If the Englishman transforms men into hats, the German transforms hats into ideas. The Englishman is Ricardo, a rich banker and distinguished economist; the German is Hegel, a simple professor of philosophy at the Berlin University.

Louis XV., the last absolute monarch and who represented the decadence of French royalty, had attached to his person a physician who was, himself, the first economist of France. This physician, this economist, represented the imminent and certain triumph of the French bourgeoisie. Doctor Quesnay has made of political economy a science; he has summarised it in his famous " Tableau Economique." Besides the thousand and one commentaries which have appeared on this

THE METAPHYSICS OF POLITICAL ECONOMY

tableau, we possess one by the doctor himself. It is, "The Analysis of the Economic Tableau," followed by " Seven Important Observations."

M. Proudhon is another Doctor Quesnay. The Quesnay of the metaphysics of political economy. But metaphysics — the whole of philosophy, in fact — is summed up, according to Hegel, in the method. It will be necessary, then, for us to endeavor to elucidate the method of M. Proudhon, which is at least as obscure as the "Tableau Economique." For that purpose we will give seven observations more or less important. If Doctor Proudhon is not content with our observations, well, then, he must play Abbé Baudeau, and give "the explanation of the economico-metaphysical method" himself.

First Observation.

" We will not make a *history according to the order of time,* but *according to the succession of ideas.* The economic *phases* or *categories* are in their *manifestation* sometimes contemporaneous, sometimes in inverse order. . . . Economic theories have also their *logical succession* and their *series in the comprehension.* It is this order which we flatter ourselves with having discovered." (Proudhon vol. I., p. 146.)

Decidedly M. Proudhon has wished to frighten the French by throwing in their faces some quasi-Hegelian phrases. We are then concerned with two men, at first with M. Proudhon and then with Hegel. How does M. Proudhon distinguish himself from other economists? And Hegel, what *rôle* does he play in the political economy of M. Proudhon?

The economists express the relation of bourgeois

THE POVERTY OF PHILOSOPHY

production, the division of labor, credit, money, &c., as categories fixed, immutable, eternal. M. Proudhon, who has before him these already formed categories, would explain to us the act of formation, the generation of these categories, principles, laws, ideas, thoughts.

The economists explain to us how production is carried on in the relation given, but what they do not explain is how these relations are produced, that is to say the historical movement which has created them. M. Proudhon, having taken these relations as abstract principles, categories, and thoughts, has only to put *order* into these thoughts, which may be found ranged alphabetically at the end of any treatise on political economy. The material of the economists is the active and busy life of men; the materials of M. Proudhon are the dogmas of the economists. But from the moment that we cease to follow the historical movement of the relations of production, of which the categories are nothing but the theoretical expression, from the moment that we see in these categories only spontaneous thoughts and ideas, independent of the real relations, we are forced to assign the movement of pure reason as the origin of these thoughts and ideas. *How does pure reason, eternal, impersonal, give birth to these thoughts? How does it proceed in order to produce them?

If we had the intrepidity of M. Proudhon in this Hegelianism we should say: Reason is distinguished in itself from itself. What does this expression mean? Impersonal reason having outside of itself neither ground upon which to stand, nor object to which it can be opposed, nor subject with which it can be composed, finds itself forced to make a somersault in posing, opposing and composing itself—position, opposition, composition. To speak Greek, we have the thesis, the antithesis

THE METAPHYSICS OF POLITICAL ECONOMY

and the synthesis. As to those who are not acquainted with Hegelian language, we would say to them in the sacramental formula, affirmation, negation, and negation of the negation. That is what it means to speak in this way. It is certainly not Hebrew, so as not to displease M. Proudhon; but it is the language of this reason so pure, separated from the individual. Instead of the ordinary individual, with his ordinary manner of speaking and thinking, we have nothing but this ordinary manner pure and simple, minus the individual.

Is there occasion to be surprised that everything, in the final abstraction, because it is abstraction and not analysis, presents itself in the state of logical category? Is there need to be astonished that in casting down little by little all which constitutes the individuality of a house, that in making abstraction of the materials of which it is composed, of the form which distinguishes it, you would come to have nothing but a body—that in making abstraction of the limits of this body you would very soon have nothing but an empty space—that, finally, in making abstraction of the dimensions of this space you would finish by having nothing more than quantity pure and simple, the logical category? In consequence of thus abstracting all the so-called accidents, animate or inanimate, men or things, we are right in saying that in the final abstraction we have as substance the logical categories. Thus the metaphysicians who imagine that in making these abstractions they make an analysis, and who in proportion as they detach more and more from certain objects imagine that they approach the point of penetrating them, these metaphysicians have in their turn the right to say that the things of this earth are embroideries of which the logical categories form the canvas. That is what distinguishes the philosopher from

THE POVERTY OF PHILOSOPHY

the Christian. The Christian has but one incarnation of the *Logos,* in spite of logic; the philosopher has never finished with incarnations. That all which exists, that all which lives on land and in water, may, by force of abstraction, be reduced to a logical category; that in this fashion the whole of the real world may be drowned in the world of abstractions, in the world of logical categories, who can wonder?

All that exists, all that lives on land and in water, exists, lives, only by some movement. Thus the movement of history produces the social relations, the industrial movement gives us the products of industry, &c.

As by the force of abstraction we have transformed everything into a logical category, so we have only to make abstraction of all distinctive character of the different movements in order to arrive at movement in the abstract, movement purely formal, at the purely logical formula of movement. If in the logical categories is found the substance of all things, it might be supposed that in the logical formula of movement would be found the *absolute method* which not only explains everything, but which further implies the movement of things.

It is of this absolute method that Hegel speaks in these terms: " Method is absolute force, unique, supreme, infinite, which no object can resist; it is the tendency of reason to find itself, to recognise itself, in everything." ("Logic," vol. III.) Everything being reduced to a logical category, and every movement, every act of production, to method, it naturally follows that all masses of products and of production, of objects and of movement, are reduced to an applied metaphysic. What Hegel has done for religion, right, &c., M. Proudhon seeks to do for political economy.

THE METAPHYSICS OF POLITICAL ECONOMY

What, then, is this absolute method? The abstraction of movement. What is the abstraction of movement? Movement in the abstract. What is movement in the abstract? The purely logical formula of movement or the movement of pure reason. In what does the movement of pure reason consist? To pose, oppose and compose itself, to be formulated as thesis, antithesis and synthesis, or, better still, to affirm itself, to deny itself and to deny its negation.

How does reason act, in order to affirm itself, to place itself in a given category? That is the affair of reason itself and its apologists.

But once it has placed itself in thesis, this thesis, this thought, opposed to itself, doubles itself into two contradictory thoughts, the positive and the negative, the yes and no. The struggle of these two antagonistic elements, comprised in the antithesis, constitutes the dialectic movement. The yes becoming no, the no becoming yes, the yes becoming at once yes and no, the no becoming at once no and yes, the contraries balance themselves, neutralise themselves, paralyse themselves. The fusion of these two contradictory thoughts constitutes a new thought which is the synthesis of the two. This new thought unfolds itself again in two contradictory thoughts which are confounded in their turn in a new synthesis. From this travail is born a group of thoughts. This group of thoughts follows the same dialectic movement as a simple category, and has for antithesis a contradictory group. From these two groups is born a new group of thoughts which is the synthesis of them.

As from the dialectic movement of simple categories is born the group, so from the dialectic movement of the

THE POVERTY OF PHILOSOPHY

groups is born the series, and from the dialectic movement of the series is born the whole system.

Apply this method to the categories of political economy, and you will have the logic and the metaphysics of political economy, or, in other words, you will have the economic categories, known to all the world, translated into an almost unknown language, which will give them the appearance of having been freshly hatched in a head of pure reason, so much do these categories seem to engender the one the other, to enchain and entangle the one in the other by the sole labor of the dialectic movement. Let not the reader be alarmed by these metaphysics with all their scaffolding of categories, of groups, of series and of systems. M. Proudhon, in spite of the great trouble he has taken to scale the height of the *system of contradictions,* has never been able to raise himself above the two first steps of simple thesis and antithesis, and yet he has bestridden them twice only, and out of the twice he has once tumbled backwards.

Up to the present we have only explained the dialectic of Hegel. We will see later how M. Proudhon has succeeded in reducing it to the most paltry proportions. Thus for Hegel, all which has passed and which still passes is exactly that which passes in his own reasoning. Thus the philosophy of history is only the history of philosophy, of his own philosophy. There is no longer "history according to the order of time"; there is only "the succession of ideas in the understanding." He thinks to construct the world by the movement of thought, while all that he does is to reconstruct systematically, and range under the absolute method, the thoughts which are in the heads of everybody.

118

THE METAPHYSICS OF POLITICAL ECONOMY

Second Observation.

The economic categories are only the theoretical expressions, the abstractions, of the social relations of production. M. Proudhon, as a true philosopher, taking the things inside out, sees in the real relations only the incarnations of these principles, of these categories, which sleep—M. Proudhon the philosopher tells us again—in the bosom of "the impersonal reason of humanity." M. Proudhon the economist has clearly understood that men make cloth, linen, silk-stuffs, in certain determined relations of production. But what he has not understood is that these determined social relations are as much produced by men as are the cloth, the linen, &c. The social relations are intimately attached to the productive forces. In acquiring new productive forces men change their mode of production, and in changing their mode of production, their manner of gaining a living, they change all their social relations. The windmill gives you society with the feudal lord; the steam-mill, society with the industrial capitalist.

The same men who establish social relations conformably with their material productivity, produce also the principles, the ideas, the categories, conformably with their social relations.

Thus these ideas, these categories, are not more eternal than the relations which they express. They are *historical and transitory products.*

There is a continual movement of growth in the productive forces, of destruction in the social relations, of formation in ideas; there is nothing immutable but the abstraction of the movement—*mors immortalis.*

THE POVERTY OF PHILOSOPHY

Third Observation.

The relations of production of every society form a whole. M. Proudhon regards the economic relations as so many phases, engendering the one the other, resulting the one from the other, as the antithesis from the thesis, and realising in their logical succession the impersonal reason of humanity.

The sole inconvenience of this method is that in approaching the examination of a single one of these phases M. Proudhon cannot explain it without having recourse to all the other relations of society, relations, however, which he has not yet caused to be engendered by his dialectic movement. When afterwards, by means of pure reason, M. Proudhon passes to the birth of the other phases, he acts as if these were new-born infants, he forgets that they are the same age as the first.

Thus, in order to arrive at the constitution of value, which is for him the basis of all the economic evolutions, he cannot get away from the division of labor, competition, &c. Nevertheless, in the *series,* in the *understanding* of M. Proudhon, in the *logical succession,* these relations do not yet exist.

In constructing with the categories of political economy the edifice of an ideological system, the members of the social system are dislocated. The different members of society are changed as belonging to separate societies which arrive one after the other. How, indeed, can the single logical formula of movement, of succession, of time, explain the composition of society, in which all the relations co-exist simultaneously and support each other?

THE METAPHYSICS OF POLITICAL ECONOMY

Fourth Observation.

Let us see now the modifications to which M. Proudhon subjects the dialectic of Hegel in applying it to political economy.

For him, M. Proudhon, every economic category has two sides, the one good, the other bad. He regards the categories as the lower middle-class regard the great men of history: Napoleon was a great man; he did very much good, he also did much evil.

The *good side* and the *bad side,* the *advantage* and the *inconvenience,* taken together, form for M. Proudhon the *contradiction* in each economic category.

The problem to solve: To conserve the good side while eliminating the bad.

Slavery is an economic category as well as any other. That then has, that also, its two sides. Let us leave the bad side and speak of the beautiful side of slavery; being understood that it is only a question of direct slavery, of the slavery of the blacks in the East, in Brazil, in the Southern States of North America.

Direct slavery is the pivot of bourgeois industry as well as machinery, credit, &c. Without slavery you have no cotton, without cotton you cannot have modern industry. It is slavery which has given their value to the colonies, it is the colonies which have created the commerce of the world, it is the commerce of the world which is the essential condition of the great industry. Thus slavery is an economic category of the highest importance.

Without slavery, North America, the most progessive country, would have been transformed into a patriarchal country. Efface North America from the map of the world and you would have the anarchy, the complete

THE POVERTY OF PHILOSOPHY

decadence, of modern commerce and civilisation. Cause slavery to disappear, and you will have effaced America from the map of nations.

Thus slavery, because it is an economic category, has always existed in the institutions of the nations. Modern nations have known how to disguise slavery in their own lands alone, they have imposed it without disguise on the New World.

What will M. Proudhon do to save slavery? He puts the problem: Conserve the good side of this economic category, eliminate the bad.

Hegel has no problems to put. He has only dialectic. M. Proudhon has of the dialectic of Hegel nothing but the language. His dialectic movement for him is the dogmatic distinction of good and evil.

Let us for an instant take M. Proudhon himself as a category. Let us examine his good and his bad side, his advantages and his inconveniences.

If he has the advantage over Hegel of putting problems which he reserves it to himself to solve for the greater good of humanity, he has the inconvenience of being stricken with sterility when it is a question of engendering by dialectical travail a new category. In order merely to put the problem of eliminating the evil side, one cuts short the dialectic movement. It is not the category which poses and opposes itself by its contradictory nature, it is M. Proudhon who disturbs himself, argues with himself, strives and struggles between the two sides of the category.

Taken thus in a impasse, from which it is difficult to escape by legitimate means, M. Proudhon performs a veritable somersault which carries him at a single bound into a new category. It is then that the series in the understanding unveils itself to his astonished eyes.

THE METAPHYSICS OF POLITICAL ECONOMY

He takes the first category to hand and arbitrarily attributes to it the quality of becoming a remedy to the inconveniences of the category which he wishes to purify. Thus imposts, if we are to believe M. Proudhon, remedy the inconveniences of monopoly; the balance of commerce, the inconveniences of imposts; landlordism, the inconveniences of credit.

In thus taking successively the economic categories one by one and making one the antidote of the other, M. Proudhon makes of this mixture of contradictions and of antidotes to the contradictions, two volumes of contradictions which he calls by their proper title: "The System of Economic Contradictions."

Fifth Observation.

"In absolute reason all these ideas .... are equally simple and general..... In fact, we attain to the science only by a kind of scaffolding of our ideas. But truth in itself is independent of its dialectical figures, and free from the combinations of our mind." (Proudhon, vol. II., p. 97.)

There at a blow, by a kind of quick change of which we now know the secret, the metaphysic of political economy becomes an illusion! Never has M. Proudhon spoken more truly. Certainly from the moment that the development of the dialectical movement is reduced to the simple process of opposing the good to the bad, of posing problems tending to eliminate the bad, and of giving one category as antidote to the other, the categories have no more spontaneity; the idea *"functions* no more," it has no longer any life in it. It no longer poses or decomposes itself in categories. The succession of categories has become a kind of *scaffolding.* The dia-

THE POVERTY OF PHILOSOPHY

lectic is no longer the movement of absolute reason. There is no longer any dialectic; at the most there is only pure ethics.

When M. Proudhon spoke of the *series in the understanding*, of the *logical succession of categories*, he declared positively that he would not give *history according to the order of time*, that is to say, according to M. Proudhon, the historical succession in which the categories are *manifested*. All therefore passed for him in the pure ether of reason. All must be caused to flow from this ether by means of dialectic. Now that it is a question of putting this dialectic in practice, reason makes default. The dialectic of M. Proudhon makes a false leap to the dialectic of Hegel, and here is M. Proudhon compelled to say that the order in which he gives the economic categories is no longer the order in which they engender each other. The economic evolutions are no longer the evolution of reason itself.

What then is it that M. Proudhon gives us? Real history, that is to say, according to the understanding of M. Proudhon, the succession in which the categories are manifested in the order of time? No. History as it passes in the idea itself? Still less that. Thus neither the profane history of categories nor their sacred history. What history does he give us, in fine? The history of his own contradictions. We will see how they march and how they draw M. Proudhon after them. Before approaching this examination, which gives place to the sixth important observation, we have still an important observation to make.

We will admit with M. Proudhon that real history, history according to the order of time, is the historical succession in which the ideas, the categories, the principles are manifested.

THE METAPHYSICS OF POLITICAL ECONOMY

Each principle has had its century in which to manifest itself. The principle of authority, for instance, had the eleventh century, as the principle of individualism had the eighteenth century. From consequence to consequence it was the century which appertained to the principle, and not the principle to the century. In other words, it was the principle which made history, it was not history which made the principle. When, further, in order to save the principles as well as history, we enquire why such a principle has been manifested in the eleventh or in the eighteenth century rather than in another, we are necessarily compelled to minutely examine into what were the men of the eleventh century, what were those of the eighteenth, what was their respective wants, their productive forces, their mode of production, the raw material of their production, in fine, what were the relations between man and man resulting from all these conditions of existence. To thoroughly examine all these questions, is it not to make real profane history of the men in each century, to represent these men at the same time as the authors and the actors of their own drama? But from the moment that you represent men as the actors and the authors of their own history you have, by a detour, arrived at the actual point of departure since you have abandoned the eternal principles from which you have at first set out.

M. Proudhon has not even advanced sufficiently on the cross-roads which the ideologist takes in order to gain the highway of history.

Sixth Observation.

Let us take with M. Proudhon this cross-road.

Let us grant that the economic relations, regarded as *immutable laws, eternal principles, ideal categories,* were

THE POVERTY OF PHILOSOPHY

anterior to active living men; that, further, these laws, these principles, these categories, had, from the beginning of time, slept "in the impersonal reason of humanity." We have already seen that with these immutable and immovable eternities, there is no history; at the most it is only history in the idea, that is to say history which is reflected in the dialectical movement of pure reason. M. Proudhon, in saying that in the dialectical movement the ideas are no longer "differentiated," has annulled both the *shadow of movement* and the *movement of the shadows*, by means of which we might at most have still created a simulacrum of history. In the place of that he imputes to history his own impotence, he takes from it all, even to the French language. "It is then not correct to say," says M. Proudhon the philosopher, "that something happens, something is *produced*: in civilisation as in the universe everything exists, everything acts from eternity. *It is thus with all social economy.*" (Vol. II., p. 102.)

Such is the productive force of the contradictions which *function* and which make M. Proudhon function, that in wishing to explain history he is forced to deny it, that in wishing to explain the successive development of social relations he denies that *anything* can happen, and in wishing to explain production in all its phases, he denies that anything can be produced.

Thus for M. Proudhon, no more history, no more succession of ideas, and nevertheless his book still exists; and this book is precisely, according to his own expression, *"history according to the succession of ideas."* How can we find a formula, as M. Proudhon is the man of formulas, by the aid of which we can leap at a single bound beyond all his contradictions?

For that he has invented a new kind of reason which

THE METAPHYSICS OF POLITICAL ECONOMY

is neither absolute reason, pure and virginal, nor the common reason of men living and active in the different centuries, but a reason quite apart, the reason of society personified, of the subject *humanity,* which, under the pen of M. Proudhon, appears sometimes also as "social genius," "general reason," and in the last place as "human reason." This reason dressed up under so many names, is, however, every instant recognised as the individual reason of M. Proudhon, with his good and bad side, his antidotes and his problems.

"Human reason does not create the truth," hidden in the profundity of absolute, eternal reason. It can only unveil it. But the truths which it has unveiled up to the present are incomplete, insufficient and therefore contradictory. Then, the economic categories, being themselves discovered truths, revealed by human reason, by social genius, are equally incomplete and enclose the germ of contradiction. Before M. Proudhon social genius has seen only the *antagonistic elements* and not the *synthetic formula,* both simultaneously hidden in *absolute reason.* Economic relations causing to be realised on earth only these insufficient truths, these incomplete categories, these contradictory notions, are then contradictory in themselves and present the two sides, of which one is good, the other evil.

To find the complete truth, the notion in all its plenitude, the synthetic formula, which will annihilate the contradiction — that is the problem of social genius. That is why still, in the illusion of M. Proudhon, the same social genius has been driven from one category to the other without having yet come, with all the battery of its categories, to drag from God, for absolute reason, a synthetic formula.

THE POVERTY OF PHILOSOPHY

"At first society (social genius) presents a first fact, emits a *hypothesis*....a true contradiction, of which the antagonistic results unfold themselves in the social economy in the same manner as the consequences would have been deduced in the mind, in such wise that the industrial movement, following in all the deductions of ideas, divides into a double current, the one of useful effects, the other of subversive results. To constitute harmoniously this two-faced principle and solve this contradiction, society develops a second, which will very soon be followed by a third; and such will be the progress of social genius until, having exhausted all its contradictions—I suppose, but that is not proved, that there is a finality to the contradiction in humanity—it returns, at a bound, upon all its anterior positions, and in a single formula solves all its problems." (Vol. I., p. 135.)

Just as before the *antithesis* was changed into the *antidote,* so now the *thesis* becomes the *hypothesis*. This change of terms on the part of M. Proudhon can no longer astonish us. Human reason which is nothing less than pure, having only incomplete views, meets at each step fresh problems to solve. Each new thesis which it discovers in absolute reason, and which is the negation of the first thesis, becomes for it a synthesis, which it naïvely accepts as the solution of the problem in question. It is thus that this reason strives with ever new contradictions, until finding itself as the end of contradictions it perceives that all its theses and syntheses are only contradictory hypotheses. In its perplexity "human reason, the social genius, returns at a bound upon all its anterior positions, and in a single formula solves all its problems." This unique formula, we may say in passing, constitutes the real discovery of M. Proudhon. It is *constituted value.*

THE METAPHYSICS OF POLITICAL ECONOMY

Hypotheses are only made in view of some end. The end proposed to itself in the first place by the social genius which speaks by the mouth of M. Proudhon, was the elimination of that which was evil in each economic category, in order to have only the good. For him good, the supreme good, the true practical end, is *equality*. And why does the social genius propose equality rather than inequality, fraternity, catholicism, or any other principle? Because "humanity has realised successively so many particular hypotheses only in view of a superior hypothesis," which is precisely equality. In other words: because equality is the ideal of M. Proudhon. He imagines that the division of labor, credit, the workshop, that all the economic relations have been invented only for the benefit of equality, and nevertheless they have always finished by turning against her. From the fact that the history and the fiction of M. Proudhon contradict each other at every step, he concludes that there is a contradiction. If there is a contradiction it exists only between his fixed idea and the real movement.

Henceforth the good side of an economic relation is that which affirms equality, the bad side is that which denies it and affirms inequality. Every new category is a hypothesis of the social genius to eliminate the inequality engendered by the preceding hypothesis. To sum up, equality is the *primitive intention*, the *mystic tendency*, the *providential end,* that the social genius has constantly before its eyes in turning round and round in the circle of economic contradictions. *Providence* is also the locomotive which conveys all the economic baggage of M. Proudhon better than his pure and heedless reason. He has devoted to Providence a whole chapter which follows that on imposts.

Providence, the providential end, that is the fine word

THE POVERTY OF PHILOSOPHY

with which we are presented to-day to explain the progress of history. In actual fact this word explains nothing. It is at most a declamatory form, one manner among others of paraphrasing the facts. It is a fact that the landed proprietors of Scotland obtained a new value by the development of English industry. This industry opened up new markets for wool. In order to produce wool on a large scale it was necessary to turn arable lands into pasture. To effect this transformation it was necessary to concentrate various properties. To concentrate these properties it was necessary to abolish small holdings, drive thousands of tenants from their native land, and put in their place a few herdsmen in charge of millions of sheep. Thus by successive transformations, landlordism in Scotland has resulted in the men being driven away by sheep. Say now that the providential end of landlordism in Scotland was to cause men to be driven away by sheep, and you have constructed providential history.

Certainly, the tendency to equality appertains to our century for the men and the means of anterior centuries with wants, means of production, &c., entirely different, worked providentially for the realisation of equality, is to begin by substituting the means and the men of one century for the men and the means of anterior centuries and to misunderstand the historical movement by which successive generations transformed the results acquired from the generations which preceded them. Economists know very well that the same thing which was for one the completed work is for the other only the raw material of further production.

Suppose, as M. Proudhon does, that the social genius has produced, or rather improvised, the feudal barons, with the providential end in view of transforming the peasants into *responsible* and *equal workmen,* and you will have made a substitution of ends and of persons quite worthy of this Providence, which in Scotland established landlordism in order to give itself the malign pleasure of substituting sheep for men.

But since M. Proudhon takes so tender an interest in Providence we will refer him to "The History of Political Economy" of M. de Villeneuve-Bargemont, who also runs after a providential end. This end is no longer equality but catholicism.

Seventh and Last Observation.

The economists have a singular manner of proceeding. There are for them only two kinds of institutions, those of art and those of nature. Feudal institutions are artificial institutions, those of the bourgeoisie are natural institutions. In this they resemble the theologians, who also establish two kinds of religion. Every religion but their own is an invention of men, while their own religion is an emanation from God. In saying that existing conditions — the conditions of bourgeois production — are natural, the economists give it to be understood that these are the relations in which wealth is created and the productive forces are developed conformably to the laws of nature. Thus these relations are themselves natural laws, independent of the influence of time. They are eternal laws which must always govern society. Thus there has been history, but there is no longer any. There has been history, since there have been feudal institutions, and in these feudal institutions were found conditions of production entirely different to those of bourgeois society, which the economists wish to have accepted as being natural and therefore eternal.

THE POVERTY OF PHILOSOPHY

Feudalism also had its proletariat—serfdom, which enclosed all the germs of the bourgeoisie. Feudal production also had two antagonistic elements, which were equally designated by the names of *good side* and *bad side* of feudalism, without regard being had to the fact that it is always the evil side which finishes by overcoming the good side. It is the bad side that produces the movement which makes history, by constituting the struggle. If at the epoch of the reign of feudalism the economists, enthusiastic over the virtues of chivalry, the delightful harmony between rights and duties, the patriarchal life of the towns, the prosperous state of domestic industry in the country, of the development of industry organised in corporations, guilds and fellowships, in fine of all which constitutes the beautiful side of feudalism, had proposed to themselves the problem of eliminating all which cast a shadow upon this lovely picture—serfdom, privilege, anarchy—what would have been the result? All the elements which constituted the struggle would have been annihilated, and the development of the bourgeoisie would have been stifled in the germ. They would have set themselves the absurd problem of eliminating history.

When the bourgeoisie had overcome it, it was no longer a question of either the good or the bad side of feudalism. The productive forces which were developed by the bourgeoisie under feudalism had now been acquired by the bourgeoisie itself. All the old economic forms, the civil relations corresponding to them, the political state which was the official expression of the old civil society, were all broken down.

Thus, in order to fairly judge feudal production, it is necessary to consider it as a system of production based on antagonism. It is necessary to show how wealth was

THE METAPHYSICS OF POLITICAL ECONOMY

produced within this antagonism, how the productive forces were developed at the same time as the antagonism of classes, how one of the classes, the bad side, the inconvenience of society, continued always to grow until the material conditions necessary to its emancipation had arrived at maturity. Is it not sufficient to say that the mode of production, the relations in which the productive forces are developed, are nothing less than eternal laws, but that they correspond to a determined development of men and of their productive forces, and that any change arising in the productive forces of men necessarily effects a change in their conditions of production? As it is above all important not to be deprived of the fruits of civilisation, of acquired productive forces, it is necessary to break the traditional forms in which they have been produced. From the moment this happens the revolutionary class becomes conservative.

The bourgeoisie commences with a proletariat which is itself a remnant of feudal times. In the course of its historical development, the bourgeoisie necessarily develops its antagonistic character, which at its first appearance was found to be more or less disguised, and existed only in a latent state. In proportion as the bourgeoisie develops, it develops in its bosom a new proletariat, a modern proletariat: it develops a struggle between the proletarian class and the bourgeois class, a struggle which, before it is felt, perceived, appreciated, comprehended, avowed and loudly proclaimed by the two sides, only manifests itself previously by partial and momentary conflicts, by subversive acts. On the other hand, if all the members of the modern bourgeoise have an identity of interest, inasmuch as they form a class opposed by another class, they have also conflicting, antagonistic interests, inasmuch as they find themselves

THE POVERTY OF PHILOSOPHY

opposed by each other. This opposition of interests flows from the economic conditions of their bourgeois life. From day to day it becomes more clear that the relations of production in which the bourgeoisie exists have not a single, a simple character, but a double character, a character of duplicity; that in the same relations in which wealth is produced, poverty is produced also; that in the same relations in which there is a development of productive forces, there is a productive force of repression; that these relations produce *bourgeois wealth*, that is to say the wealth of the bourgeois class, only in continually annihilating the wealth of integral members of that class and in producing an ever-growing proletariat.

The more this antagonistic character comes to light the more the economists, the scientific representatives of bourgeois production, become excited with their own theories, and different schools are formed.

We have the *fatalist* economists, who in their theory are as indifferent to what they call the inconveniences of bourgeois production, as the bourgeois themselves are, in actual practice, to the sufferings of the proletarians who assist them to acquire riches. In this fatalist school there are classicists and romanticists. The classicists, like Adam Smith and Ricardo, represent a bourgeoisie which, still struggling with the relics of feudal society, labors only to purify economic relations from the feudal blemishes, to augment the productive forces, and to give to industry and to commerce a fresh scope. The proletariat participating in this struggle, absorbed in this feverish labor, has only passing accidental sufferings to endure, and itself regards them as such. Economists like Adam Smith and Ricardo, who are the

THE METAPHYSICS OF POLITICAL ECONOMY

historians of this epoch, have no other mission than to demonstrate how wealth is acquired in the relations of bourgeois production, to formulate these relations in categories, in laws, and to demonstrate how far these laws, these categories, are, for the production of wealth, superior to the laws and categories of feudal society. Poverty in their eyes is only the pain which accompanies all child-birth, in nature as well as in industry.

The romanticists appertain to our epoch, where the bourgeoisie is in direct antagonism to the proletariat; where poverty is engendered in as great abundance as wealth. The economists then pose as satisfied fatalists who, from their lofty position, throw a glance of superb disdain on the active men who manufacture wealth. They copy all the developments given by their predecessors, and the indifference with which those was naïveté becomes for these others mere coquetry.

Afterwards comes the *humanitarian* school, which takes to heart the evil side of the existing relations of production. This school seeks, as an acquittal for its conscience, to palliate, however little, existing contrasts; it sincerely deplores the distress of the proletariat, the unrestricted competition between the bourgeoisie themselves; it advises the workers to be sober and industrious, and to have but few children; it recommends the bourgeoisie to put thoughtful earnestness into the work of production. The whole theory of this school rests upon interminable distinctions between theory and practice, between principles and results, between the idea and the application, between the content and the form, between the essence and the reality, between right and fact, between the good and the evil side.

The philanthropic school is the humanitarian school

THE POVERTY OF PHILOSOPHY

perfected. It denies the necessity of antagonism; it would make all men bourgeois; it would realise the theory in so far as it is distinguished from practice and encloses no antagonism. It goes without saying that, in theory, it is easy to make abstraction of the contradictions that are met with each instant in reality. This theory would become then idealised reality. The philanthropists thus wish to conserve the categories which express bourgeois relations, without having the antagonism which is inseparable from these relations. They fancy they are seriously combatting the bourgeois system, and they are more bourgeois than the others.

As the economists are the scientific representatives of the bourgeois class, so the Socialists and Communists are the theorists of the proletarian class. So long as the proletariat is not sufficiently developed to constitute itself as a class, so long as, in consequence, the struggle between the proletariat and the bourgeoisie has not acquired a political character, and while the productive forces are not sufficiently developed in the bosom of the bourgeoisie itself to allow a perception of the material conditions necessary to the emancipation of the proletariat and the formation of a new society, so long these theorists are only utopians who, to obviate the distress of the oppressed classes, improvise systems and run after a regenerative science. But as history develops and with it the struggle of the proletariat becomes more clearly defined, they have no longer any need to seek for such a science in their own minds, they have only to give an account of what passes before their eyes and to make of that their medium. So long as they seek science and only make systems, so long as they are at the beginning of the struggle, they see in poverty only poverty, without seeing therein the revolutionary subversive side which will overturn the old society. From that moment science, produced by the historical movement and linking itself thereto in full knowledge of the facts of the case, has ceased to be doctrinaire and has become revolutionary.

Let us return to M. Proudhon.

Each economic relation has a good and bad side: that is the single point upon which M. Proudhon does not contradict himself. The good side, he sees explained by the economists; the bad side, he sees denounced by the Socialists. He borrows from the economists the necessity of eternal relations; he borrows from the Socialists the illusion of seeing in poverty only poverty. He is in agreement with both in wishing to refer it to the authority of science. Science, for him, is reduced to the insignificant proportion of a scientific formula. It is thus that M. Proudhon flatters himself to have made the criticism of both political economy and of communism: he is below both the one and the other. Below the economists, since as a philosopher, who has under his hand a magic formula, he has believed himself able to do without entering into purely economic details; below the Socialists, since he has neither sufficient courage nor sufficient intelligence to raise himself, were it only speculatively, above the bourgeois horizon.

He wished to be the synthesis, he is a composite error.

He wished to soar as man of science above the bourgeoisie and the proletarians; he is only the petty bourgeois, tossed about constantly between capital and labor, between political economy and communism.

Section II.— The Division of Labor and Machinery.

The division of labor opens, according to M. Proudhon, the series of economic evolutions.

The good side of the division of labor.	"Considered in its essence, the division of labor is the mode according to which is realised the equality of conditions and of intelligences." (Vol. I., p. 93.)
The bad side of the division of labor.	"The division of labor has become for us an instrument of misery." (Vol. I., p. 99.) Variant. "Labor, in *dividing itself according to the law* which belongs to it, and which is the first condition of its fecundity, tends to the negation of its ends, and destroys itself." (Vol. I., p. 94.)
The problem to solve.	To find "the recomposition which will efface the inconveniences of the division of labor while conserving all its useful effects." (Vol. I., p. 97.)

The division of labor is, according to M. Proudhon, an eternal law, a simple and abstract category. It is

THE METAPHYSICS OF POLITICAL ECONOMY

necessary, then, that the abstraction, the idea, the word, should suffice him to explain the division of labor in the different epochs of history. Castes, corporations, the manufacturing *régime,* the great industry, must be explained by the single word *division.* First study well the meaning of division, and then you will not need to study the numerous influences which give to the division of labor a definite character in each epoch.

Certainly this would be to render things altogether too simple, by merely reducing them to the categories of M. Proudhon. History does not proceed so categorically. Three whole centuries have been necessary in Germany to establish the first great division of labor — that is, the separation of the town from the country. As this single relation, that of town to country, became modified, so the whole society was modified in consequence. To view only this single phase of the division of labor you have the ancient Republics, or Christian feudalism; early England with its barons, or modern England with its cotton-lords. In the fourteenth and fifteenth centuries, when yet there were no colonies, when America did not yet exist for Europe, when Asia only existed by the intermediary of Constantinople, when the Mediterranean was the centre of commercial activity, the division of labor had quite another form, quite another aspect, to that which it had in the seventeenth century, when the Spaniards, the Portuguese, the English, and the French had colonies established in all parts of the world. The extent of the market, and its physiognomy, give to the division of labor in the different epochs a physiognomy, a character, which it would be difficult to deduce from the single word division, from the idea, or from the category.

" All the economists," says M. Proudhon, " since Adam Smith have designated the *advantages* and the *incon-*

THE POVERTY OF PHILOSOPHY

veniences of the law of division, but have insisted very much more on the first than on the second, because that better served their optimism, and without any one of them ever asking himself what could be the inconveniences of a law...... How could the same principle, pursued rigorously to its consequences, conduct to effects diametrically opposed? No single economist, either before or since Adam Smith, has done more than perceive that there was a problem to solve. Say only goes so far as to recognise that in the division of labor the same cause which produces the good engenders the evil."

Adam Smith goes farther than M. Proudhon thinks he does. He has clearly seen that "in reality the difference of natural talents between individuals is much less than is supposed. These dispositions so different, which seem to distinguish the men of different professions when they arrive at mature age, are not so much the *cause* as the *effect* of the division of labor." In principle a porter differs less from a philosopher than a mastiff from a greyhound. It is the division of labor which has placed an abyss between the two. All this does not prevent M. Proudhon from saying, in another place, that Adam Smith had no doubt of the inconveniences produced by the division of labor. It is still this which makes him say that J. B. Say was the *first* to recognise "that in the division of labor the same cause which produces the good engenders the evil."

But let us hear Lemontey: *suum cuique*. "M. J. B. Say has done me the honor of adopting in his excellent treatise on political economy the principle *which I brought to light* in this fragment on the moral influence of the division of labor. The somewhat frivolous title of my book has doubtless precluded him from citing me.

THE METAPHYSICS OF POLITICAL ECONOMY

I can attribute to no other motive than this the silence of a writer too rich in his own treasures to need to disavow so modest a loan." (Lemontey, "Œuvres Complètes," Vol. I., p. 245, Paris, 1840.)

Let us render him this justice: Lemontey has intellectually explained the evil consequences of the division of labor, as it is constituted in our days, and M. Proudhon found nothing to add thereto. But since, by the faults of M. Proudhon, we are now engaged in this question of priority, we may say in passing that long before M. Lemontey, and seventeen years before Adam Smith, the pupil of A. Ferguson, the latter clearly explained the subject in a chapter treating specially of the division of labor.

"There will ever be doubts as to whether the general capacity of a nation grows in proportion to the progress of the arts. Many mechanical arts.... succeed perfectly when they are totally destitute of the assistance of reason or sentiment, and ignorance is the mother of industry as well as of superstition. Reflection and imagination are likely to go astray, but the habit of moving the hand or foot depends upon neither the one or the other. Thus, we might say that perfection, as regards manufacture, consists in its being able to be dismissed from the mind, in such a manner that without an effort of the brain the workshop may be operated like a machine, of which the parts are men.... The general officer may be very accomplished in the art of war while all the merit of the soldier is limited to executing certain movements of the foot or hand. The one may have gained what the other has lost..... In a period where all is separated, the art of thinking may itself form a separate function." (A. Ferguson, "Essai sur l'histoire de la Socété Civile," Paris, 1783.)

THE POVERTY OF PHILOSOPHY

To terminate the literary view, we formally deny that "*all* the economists have insisted very much more on the advantages than on the inconveniences of the division of labor." It is sufficient to name Sismondi.

Thus, as regards the *advantages* of the division of labor, M. Proudhon had nothing to do but to paraphrase, more or less pompously, the general phrases which everybody knows.

Let us now see how he derives from the division of labor, taken as a general law, as a category, a thought, the inconveniences which are attached to it. How is it that this category, this law, implies an unequal distribution of labor to the detriment of the equalitarian system of M. Proudhon?

" At this solemn hour of the division of labor the wind of the tempests begins to beat upon humanity. Progress is not accomplished for all in an equal and uniform manner; . . . it begins by creating a small number of privileged persons. . . . It is this respect of persons on the part of progress which has created the old-established belief in the natural and providential inequality of conditions, and has given birth to castes, and has hierarchically constituted all societies." (Proudhon, Vol. I, p. 97.)

The division of labor has made castes. But castes are the inconveniences of the division of labor; then it is the division of labor which has engendered inconveniences. *Quod erat demonstrandum.* Would you go further and ask what causes the division of labor to create castes, hierarchic constitutions and privileged classes? M. Proudhon will tell you: Progress. And what has made this progress? The limit. The limit for M. Proudhon is the respect of persons on the part of progress.

After philosophy comes history. This is no longer

either descriptive history or dialectic history, it is comparative history. M. Proudhon establishes a comparison between the workman printer of to-day and the workman printer of the Middle Ages; between the workman of the Creusot ironworks and the country blacksmith; between the man of letters of our days and the man of letters of the Middle Ages; and he makes the balance lean to the side of those who appertain more or less to the division of labor such as the Middle Ages have constituted or transmitted it. He opposes the division of labor of one historical epoch to the division of labor of another historical epoch. Was this what M. Proudhon had to demonstrate? No. He ought to have shown us the inconveniences of the division of labor in general, of the division of labor as category. But of what use is it further to dwell upon this part of M. Proudhon's work, since a little further on we shall see him formally retract all these pretended developments himself?

"The first effect of divided labor," continues M. Proudhon, "after the *degradation of the mind,* is the prolongation of the periods of work, which grow in inverse ratio to the amount of intelligence exercised. . . . But, as the duration of these periods cannot exceed sixteen or eighteen hours a day, from the moment when compensation cannot be taken by additional time it will be effected in the price, and wages will fall. . . . This is certain — and that is all we are concerned to note — that the *universal conscience* does not put at the same rate the work of an overseer and that of a laborer. There is, then, a necessity for a reduction in the price of the day's work, so that the worker, after having been afflicted in his mind by a degrading function, should not fail to be also stricken in the body by the meagreness of the remuneration."

THE POVERTY OF PHILOSOPHY

We will pass over the logical value of these syllogisms, which Kant would call paralogisms, and consider them as they are.

Here is their substance:

The division of labor reduces the worker to a degrading function; to this degrading function corresponds a depraved mind; with the depravity of the mind goes a constant reduction of wages. And, in order to prove that this reduction of wages is adapted to a depraved mind, M. Proudhon says, to absolve his own conscience, that it is the universal conscience which wills it thus. Is the soul of M. Proudhon counted in the universal conscience?

Machinery is, for M. Proudhon, "the logical antithesis of the division of labor," and, in support of his dialectic he begins by transforming machinery into a factory.

After having supposed the modern factory in order to have poverty flow from the division of labor, M. Proudhon supposes poverty engendered by the division of labor in order to arrive at the factory, and to be able to represent it as the dialectic negation of this poverty. After having stricken the worker morally by a degrading function, and physically by the meagreness of his wages, after having put the worker in a position of dependence upon the overseer and reduced his work to the mere manual task of a laborer, he betakes himself again to the factory and to the machines in order to *degrade* the worker by "giving him a *master*," and he finishes his humiliation by causing him to be "reduced from the rank of an artisan to that of a mere laborer." What beautiful dialectic! And yet if he would only stick to that! But no, he must have a new history of the division of labor, no longer in order to derive contradictions therefrom, but in order to reconstruct the factory after his own fashion. To arrive at this end he has to forget all that he has just said about this division.

Labor is organised, and divided, variously, according to the instruments which it manipulates. The windmill supposes a division of labor quite other than that of the steam mill. To begin by the division of labor in general in order to arrive at a specific instrument of production, machinery, is therefore to fly in the face of history.

Machinery is no more an economic category than is the ox which draws the plough. Machinery is only a productive force. The modern workshop, which is based on the application of machinery, is a social relation of production, an economic category.

Let us see now how these things pass in the brilliant imagination of M. Proudhon.

"In society the incessant apparition of machinery is the antithesis, the inverse formula, of labor; it is the protest of industrial genius against fragmentary *and homicidal labor*. What, in effect, is a machine? *A means of reuniting different particles of labor,* which division had separated. Every machine might be defined as a summary of many operations..... Therefore, through the machine, there would be the *restoration of the worker*..... Machinery standing in political economy in contradiction to the division of labor, represents the synthesis, opposing, in the human mind, the analysis.... The division only separates the different parts of labor, leaving each to the speciality most agreeable to him: The factory groups the workers, according to the relation of each part to the whole .... it introduces the principle of authority into labor..... But that is not all: The machine or the factory, after having degraded the workman by giving him a master, finishes his humiliation by

THE POVERTY OF PHILOSOPHY

causing him to be reduced from the rank of an artisan to that of a mere laborer. . . . The period through which we are now passing, that of machinery, is distinguished by a special character, it is that of the *wage-worker*. The wage-worker is posterior to the division of labor and exchange."

A simple observation to M. Proudhon. The separation of the different parts of labor, leaving to each man the faculty of devoting himself to the specialty most agreeable to him, a separation which M. Proudhon dates from the beginning of the world, exists only in modern industry, under the *régime* of competition.

M. Proudhon afterwards gives us a " genealogy," much too " interesting," in order to demonstrate how the workshop is born from the division of labor and the wage-worker from the workshop.

1. He imagines a man who " has remarked that by dividing production into different parts, and causing each to be executed by a separate workman," the forces of production might be multiplied.

2. This man, seizing the thread of this idea, " tells himself that in forming a permanent group of assorted workmen for the special object that he has in view, he will obtain a more regular and more abundant production, &c."

3. This man makes a *proposition* to other men to get them to grasp his idea, and the thread of his idea.

4. This man, at the inception of the industry, acts as an equal to equals towards the companions who, later, become his workmen.

5. " He is sensible, in fact, that this primitive equality must rapidly disappear through the advantageous position of the master and the dependence of the wage-worker."

THE METAPHYSICS OF POLITICAL ECONOMY

That is a further sample of the *historical and descriptive* method of M. Proudhon.

Let us now examine, from the historical and economic point of view, and see if really the workshop or the machine has introduced the *principle of authority* into society subsequent to the division of labor; if it has on one hand rehabilitated the worker, while on the other subjecting him to authority; if the machine is the recomposition of divided labor, the *synthesis* of labor opposed to its *analysis*.

Society as a whole has this in common with the interior of a factory, that it also has its division of labor. If the division of labor in a modern factory, were taken as a model to be applied to an entire society, the society the best organised for the production of wealth would be incontestably that which had but one single master distributing the work, according to a regulation arranged beforehand, to the various members of the community. But it is not so. While in the interior of the modern factory the division of labor is minutely regulated by the authority of the capitalist, modern society has no other regulation, no other authority, to arrange the distribution of labor, than free competition.

Under the patriarchal *régime,* under the *régime* of castes, under the feudal and corporative *régime,* there was division of labor in the whole of society according to fixed regulations. Were these regulations established by a legislator? No. Originally born of the conditions of material production, it was not till much later that they were established as laws. It was thus that these various forms of the division of labor became to such an extent the bases of social organisation. As to the division of labor in the factory, it was very little developed in all these forms of society.

THE POVERTY OF PHILOSOPHY

It might even be set up as a general rule, that the less authority presides over the division of labor in the interior of society, the more will the division of labor be developed inside the factory and the more absolutely will it there be subject to the authority of a single individual. Thus the authority in the factory and that in society, in relation to the division of labor, are in inverse ratio the one to the other.

It is now important to see what is this factory, in which the occupations are greatly separated, where the task of each worker is reduced to a very simple operation, and where the authority, capital, groups and directs the laborers. How has this workshop come into existence? To answer this question we shall have to examine how manufacturing industry, properly so-called, has been developed. I refer now to that industry which is not yet modern industry, with its machinery, but which is, at the same time, neither the industry of the artisans of the Middle Ages nor domestic industry. We will not enter into elaborate details; we will only give some summarised points in order to show that history cannot be made with formulas.

One of the most indispensable conditions for the formation of the manufacturing industry was the accumulation of capitals facilitated by the discovery of America and the introduction of its precious metals.

It has been sufficiently proved that the augmentation of the means of exchange has resulted in, on one side the depreciation of wages and rent, and on the other the increase of industrial profits. In other terms, in proportion as the landlord class and the working class, the feudal lords and the people, fall, so the capitalists class, the bourgeoisie, rises.

THE METAPHYSICS OF POLITICAL ECONOMY

There have been other circumstances which have operated simultaneously with the development of the manufacturing industry—the increase of the commodities put in circulation when commerce penetrated to the East Indies by way of the Cape of Good Hope, the colonial *régime,* and the development of maritime commerce.

Another point which has not yet been sufficiently appreciated in the history of manufacturing industry was the disbanding of the numerous retainers of the feudal lords, the subaltern members of which became vagabonds before entering the factory. The creation of the factory was preceded by an almost universal vagabondage in the fifteenth and sixteenth centuries. The factory found another powerful support in the numerous peasants, who, continually driven from the country districts by the transformation of the fields into pasturage, and through the progress of agriculture rendering a smaller number of hands necessary for cultivation, steadily flocked into the towns during whole centuries.

The growth of the market, the accumulation of capitals, the modification in the social position of classes, a crowd of people who found themselves deprived of their sources of income, these were the various historical conditions for the formation of the manufacturing industry. It was not, as M. Proudhon says, certain amiable stipulations between equals which brought men together in the factory. It was not even in the bosom of the ancient corporations that manufacture had its birth. It was the merchant who became the chief of the modern factory, and not the ancient master of corporations. Almost everywhere there was a furious struggle between the manufacturing industry and the handicrafts.

The accumulation and concentration of instruments of production and of workpeople preceded the development

THE POVERTY OF PHILOSOPHY

of the division of labor inside the factory. A manufactory consists very much more in the union of a large number of workpeople and many trades in a single place, in one apartment, under the control of one capital, than in the analysis of the different operations and the adaptation of each worker to one simple task.

The utility of a factory consists much less in the division of labor, properly so-called, than in the fact that the work is performed on a much larger scale, that much unproductive expenditure is thereby saved, &c. At the end of the sixteenth and the beginning of the seventeenth centuries, there was scarcely any division of labor in Dutch manufactories.

The development of the division of labor presupposes the union of workpeople in a factory. There is not even a single example, either in the sixteenth or seventeenth centuries, of the different branches of the same trade being separately exploited to such a point that it would have sufficed to bring them together in one place to obtain a complete factory. But once the men and the instruments of production were brought together, the division of labor, as it existed under the form of co-operation, was reproduced, was necessarily reflected, inside the factory.

For M. Proudhon, who sees things upside down, if indeed he always sees them, the division of labor, in the sense given to it by Adam Smith, preceded the factory which was a necessary condition of its existence.

Machinery properly so-called dates from the end of the eighteenth century. Nothing could be more absurd than to see in machinery the *antithesis* of the division of labor, the *synthesis* giving unity again to divided labor.

The machine is a union of the instruments of labor,

THE METAPHYSICS OF POLITICAL ECONOMY

and not at all a combination of labors for the workman himself. "When, by the division of labor, each separate operation has been reduced to the operation of a simple instrument, the union of all these instruments, put in operation by a single motor, constitutes — a machine." (Babbage, "Traité sur l'Economie des Machines," &c., Paris, 1833.) Simple tools, accumulation of tools, composite tools, the putting in motion of a composite tool by a single manual motor, by man, the putting in motion of these instruments by natural forces, the machine, a system of machines with a single motor, a system of machines with an automaton for motor — such is the development of machinery.

The concentration of the instruments of production and the division of labor are as inseparable the one from the other as are, in the domain of politics, the concentration of the public powers and the division of private interests. England, with the concentration of land, the instrument of agricultural industry, has, at the same time, division of agricultural labor and the application of machinery to the exploitation of the soil. France which has the division of this instrument, the system of small property in land, has, generally speaking, neither division of agricultural labor nor the application of machinery to the cultivation of the soil.

For M. Proudhon the concentration of the instruments of labor is the negation of the division of labor. In reality we find it to be quite the contrary. In proportion as the concentration of these instruments is developed, so also this division is developed, and *vice versa*. To this is due the fact that every great invention in mechanics is followed by a greater division of labor, and each advance in the division of labor brings in its turn new mechanical inventions.

THE POVERTY OF PHILOSOPHY

We do not need to recall the fact that the great development of the division of labor began in England after the invention of machinery. Thus the spinners and weavers were, for the most part, peasants, such as we meet them to-day in the more backward countries. The invention of machines has completely separated the manufacturing from the agricultural industry. The spinner and the weaver, hitherto united in one family, were separated by the machine. Thanks to the machine the spinner can live in England while the weaver dwells in India. Before the invention of machinery the industry of a country was exercised principally on the raw material which was the product of its soil; thus in England wool, in Germany flax, in France silk and flax, in India and the Levant cotton, &c. Thanks to the application of machinery and of steam the division of labor has been able to assume such dimensions that the great industry, detached from the national soil, depends only upon the markets of the world, on international exchanges, and on an international division of labor. In fine, the machine exercises such an influence on the division of labor that when in the manufacture of any given product, means have been found to partially introduce mechanical appliances, the manufacture has been immediately divided into two exploitations entirely independent of each other.

Is it necessary to speak of the *providential* and philanthropic *end* which M. Proudhon discovers in the original invention and application of machinery?

When in England the market had become so fully developed that manual labor no longer sufficed to supply it, the need for machinery made itself felt. It was then that the application of mechanical science, which had been fully prepared during the eighteenth century, was thought of.

THE METAPHYSICS OF POLITICAL ECONOMY

The organised factory marked its appearance by acts which were nothing short of philanthropic. Chrildren were kept to work by blows of the whip; they were made objects of traffic, and were contracted for with orphanages and workhouses. All the laws on the apprenticeship of workpeople were abolished, because, to make use of the phrases of M. Proudhon *synthesised* workers were no longer needed. In fine, from 1825 all the new inventions were the result of conflicts between the worker and the capitalist, who sought at all costs to depreciate the speciality of the workman. After each strike, however unimportant, a new machine appeared. The workman was so far from seeing in the machines a kind of rehabilitation, of *restoration,* as M. Proudhon calls it, that, in the eighteenth century, he for a long time resisted the nascent empire of the automaton.

"Wyatt," says Doctor Ure, "invented the series of fluted rollers, the spinning fingers usually ascribed to Arkwright.".... "The main difficulty did not, to my apprehension, lie so much in the invention of a proper self-acting mechanism ..... as in training human beings to renounce their desultory habits of work, and to identify themselves with the unvarying regularity of the complex automaton. But to devise and administer a successful code of factory discipline suited to the necessities of factory diligence, was the Herculean enterprise. The whole achievement of Arkwright."

In short, by the introduction of machinery the division of labor within society has been developed, the task of the workman within the factory has been simplified, capital has been accumulated, and man has been further dismembered.

If M. Proudhon would be an economist, and leave for

THE POVERTY OF PHILOSOPHY

an instant "the evolution in the series of the understanding," he would draw from Adam Smith his knowledge of the time when the automatic factory had scarcely come into existence; in fact, learn the difference between the division of labor as it existed in the time of Adam Smith and as we see it in the automatic factory. In order to make this clearly understood it will be sufficient to cite some passages from the "Philosophy of Manufactures," by Doctor Ure: —

"When Adam Smith wrote his immortal elements of economics, automatic machinery being hardly known, he was properly led to regard the division of labor as the grand principle of manufacturing improvement; and he showed, in the example of pin-making, how each handicraftsman, being thereby enabled to perfect himself by practice in one point, became a quicker and cheaper workman. In each branch of manufacture he saw that some parts were, on that principle, of easy execution, like the cutting of pin wires into uniform lengths, and some were comparatively difficult, like the formation and fixation of their heads; and therefore he concluded that to each a workman of appropriate value and cost was naturally assigned. This appropriation forms the very essence of the division of labor. . . . But what was in Dr. Smith's time a topic of useful illustration, cannot now be used without risk of misleading the public mind as to the right principle of manufacturing industry. In fact, the division, or rather adaptation of labor to the different talents of men, is little thought of in factory employment. On the contrary, wherever a process requires peculiar dexterity and steadiness of hand it is withdrawn as soon as possible from the *cunning* workman, who is prone to irregularities of many kinds, and it is

THE METAPHYSICS OF POLITICAL ECONOMY

placed in charge of a peculiar mechanism so self-regulating that a child may superintendent it. . . . The principle of the factory system, then, is to substitute mechanical science for hand skill, and the partition of a process into its essential constituents, for the division or gradation of labor among artisans. On the handicraft plan, labor, more or less skilled, was usually the most expensive element of production — but on the automatic plan skilled labor gets progressively superseded, and will, eventually, be replaced by mere overlookers of machines. By the infirmity of human nature it happens that the more skilful the workman the more self-willed and intractable he is apt to become, and, of course, the less fit a component of a mechanical system, in which, by occasional irregularities, he may do great damage to the whole. The grand object, therefore, of the modern manufacturer is, through the union of capital and science, to reduce the task of his workpeople to the exercise of vigilance and dexterity — faculties, when concentred to one process, speedily brought to perfection in the young. . . .

"On the gradation system, a man must serve an apprenticeship of many years before his hand and eye become skilled enough for certain mechanical feats; but on the system of decomposing a process into its constituents, and embodying each part in an automatic machine, a person of common care and capacity may be entrusted with any of the said elementary parts after a short probation, and may be transferred from one to another, on any emergency, at the discretion of the master. Such translations are utterly at variance with the old practice of the division of labor, which fixed one man to shaping the head of a pin, and another to sharpening its point, with most irksome and spiritwasting uniformity for a whole life. . . . But on the equalisation plan of self-acting

THE POVERTY OF PHILOSOPHY

machines, the operative needs to call his faculties only into agreeable exercise.....

"As his business consists in tending the work of a well-regulated mechanism, he can learn it in a short period; and when he transfers his services from one machine to another, he varies his task, and enlarges his views by thinking on those general combinations which result from his and his companions' labors. Thus, that cramping of the faculties, that narrowing of the mind, that stunting of the frame, which were ascribed, and not unjustly, by moral writers, to the division of labor, cannot, in common circumstances, occur under the equable distribution of industry..... It is, in fact, the constant aim and tendency of every improvement in machinery to supersede human labor altogether, or to diminish its cost, by substituting the industry of women and children for that of men; or that of ordinary laborers for trained artisans..... This tendency to employ merely children with watchful eyes and nimble fingers, instead of journeymen of long experience, shows how the scholastic dogma of the division of labor into degrees of skill has been exploded by our enlightened manufacturers." (Andrew Ure, "Philosophy of Manufactures" (1835) pp. 15 and 16.)

That which characterises the division of labor within modern society is that it engenders specialities, species, and with them the stupefying of handicraft.

"We are struck with admiration," says Lemontey, "in seeing among the ancients the same individual being at once, and in an eminent degree, philosopher, poet, orator, historian, priest, administrator and general. Our minds are awe-stricken at the contemplation of so vast a domain. Each one now plants his hedge and fences himself within

THE METAPHYSICS OF POLITICAL ECONOMY

his own enclosure. I do not know if by this cutting up the field is extended, but I know very well that man is lessened thereby."

The division of labor in the automatic factory is characterised by this, that labor there has lost all specialised character. But from the moment that all special development ceases, the need of universality, the tendency towards an integral development of the individual begins to make itself felt. The automatic factory effaces species and the stupefying of handicraft.

M. Proudhon, not having so much as comprehended this single revolutionary side of the automatic factory, takes a step backward, and proposes to the workman that he should not only make the twelfth part of a pin, but the whole twelve parts in succession. The workman would thus arrive at the science and conscience of the pin. Such is the synthetic labor of M. Proudhon. No one can deny that to make one movement forward and another backward, is equally to make a synthetic movement.

To sum up, M. Proudhon has not got beyond the ideal of the petty bourgeois. And in order to realise this ideal he thinks of nothing better than to bring us back to the companion, or at most to the master, workman of the Middle Ages. It suffices, he says somewhere in his book, to have made a masterpiece once in a lifetime, to have felt oneself a man for once. Is not that, in its form as well as in its basis, the masterpiece exacted by the trade guild of the Middle Ages?

SECTION III.— COMPETITION AND MONOPOLY.

The good side of competition.	"Competition is as essential to labor as division. . . . It is necessary to the *advent of equality*."
The bad side of competition.	"This principle is the negation of itself. Its most certain effect is to ruin those whom it draws into its train."
General reflection.	"The *inconveniences* which follow in its train, as well as the good which it procures . . . flow logically, the one and the other, from the principle."
Problem to solve.	"To find the principle of *reconciliation*, which must be derived from a law superior to liberty itself." VARIANT. "It cannot therefore be here a question of destroying competition, a thing as impossible as to destroy liberty itself; it is a question of finding the equilibrium, I will frankly say the *police*."

M. Proudhon begins by defending the eternal necessity

THE METAPHYSICS OF POLITICAL ECONOMY

of competition against those who would replace it by *emulation.*

There is no "emulation without an object," and as "the object of every passion is necessarily analogous to the passion, a mistress for the lover, power for the ambitious, gold for the avaricious, a crown for the poet; the object of industrial emulation is necessarily *profit.* Emulation is nothing but competition itself."

Competition is emulation in view of profit. Is industrial emulation necessarily emulation in view of profit, that is to say, competition? M. Proudhon proves it in affirming it. We have already seen that to affirm is, for him, to prove, the same as to suppose is to deny.

If the immediate object of the lover is a mistress, the immediate object of industrial emulation is the product and not the profit.

Competition is not industrial emulation, it is commercial emulation. In our days industrial emulation only exists in view of commerce. There are some phases in the economic life of modern peoples in which everybody is seized with a kind of vertigo for making profit without producing. This vertigo of speculation, which reappears periodically, discloses the real character of competition which seeks to escape the necessity of industrial emulation.

If you had told an artisan of the fourteenth century that the privileges and the whole feudal organisation of industry were about to be abrogated, in order to put industrial emulation, called competition, in their place, he would have answered that the privileges of the various corporations, masters and wardens, were organised competition. M. Proudhon says no better in affirming that "emulation is nothing but competition itself."

"Enact that from January 1, 1847, work and wages

THE POVERTY OF PHILOSOPHY

shall be guaranteed to everybody: immediately an immense relaxation would succeed to the ardent tension of industry."

In the place of a supposition, an affirmation, and a negation, we have now an ordinance, which M. Proudhon gives expressly in order to prove the necessity of competition, its eternity as a category, &c.

If people were to suppose that it only requires an ordinance to escape from competition, they would never escape from it. And to go so far as to propose the abolition of competition while retaining the wage system is to propose to make nonsense by a royal decree. But the peoples do not proceed by royal decree. Before making these ordinances they have at least to change, from top to bottom, their industrial and political conditions of existence, and, in consequence, all their manner of being.

M. Proudhon would answer with his imperturbable assurance that this is the hypothesis "of a transformation of our nature without historical precedent," and that he would have the right to "put us outside the discussion" in virtue of we know not what ordinance.

M. Proudhon does not know that the whole of history is nothing but a continual transformation of human nature.

"Let us keep to facts. The French Revolution was made for industrial as well as for political liberty; and, although France, in 1789, may not have recognised all the consequences of the principle, the realisation of which she demanded, we may say frankly she was not deceived either in her desires or in her attempt. Whoever should attempt to deny this would in my opinion lose the right of criticism. I will never dispute with an adversary who would lay down as a principle that 25,000,000 of

THE METAPHYSICS OF POLITICAL ECONOMY

men had spontaneously been guilty of error..... Why, then, if competition were not a *principle* of the social economy, a *decree of destiny,* a *necessity of the human mind,* why, instead of abolishing corporations, companies and wardenships, did not people rather think of reestablishing the whole of them?"

Thus, since the French people of the eighteenth century abolished corporations, companies and wardenships, instead of modifying them, the French people of the nineteenth century ought to modify competition instead of abolishing it. Since competition was established in France, in the eighteenth century, as a consequence of historical needs, this competition must not be destroyed in the nineteenth century in consequence of other historical needs. M. Proudhon, not comprehending that the establishment of competition was bound up with the actual development of the men of the eighteenth century, makes of competition a necessity of the human mind, *in partibus infidelium.* What would he have made of the great Colbert for the seventeenth century?

After the Revolution comes the existing state of things. M. Proudhon also draws some facts from that in order to show the eternity of competition, by proving that all the industries in which this category is not yet sufficiently developed, as agriculture, are in a state of inferiority, of decay.

To say that there are some industries which are not yet at the height of competition, that yet others are below the level of bourgeois production, is mere quibbling which by no means proves the eternity of competition.

All the logic of M. Proudhon is summed up in this: Competition is a social relation in which we really develop our productive forces. He gives to this truth, not any

THE POVERTY OF PHILOSOPHY

logical developments, but certain forms, often well developed, in saying that competition is industrial emulation, the actual mode of being free, responsibility in labor, the constitution of value, a necessary condition for the future of equality, a principle of social economy, a decree of destiny, a necessity of the human mind, an inspiration of eternal justice, liberty in division, division in liberty, an economic category.

"Competition and association support each other. So far from excluding each other they are not even *divergent*. Who speaks of competition already supposes a common end. Competition therefore is not *egoism*, and the most deplorable error of Socialism lay in having regarded it as the overthrow of society."

Who speaks of competition speaks of a common end, and that proves, on the one hand, that competition is association; on the other, that competition is not egoism. And does not he who speaks of egoism, speak of a common end? Each egoism operates in society and by reason of the existence of society. It, therefore, presupposes society, that is to say common ends, common wants, common means of production, &c., &c. Can it by chance be that, therefore, the competition and the association of which the Socialists speak are not even divergent?

The Socialists know very well that modern society is based upon competition. How can they reproach competition with overthrowing the existing society, which they desire to overthrow themselves? And how can they reproach competition with the overthrow of the society of the future in which, on the contrary, they see the overthrow of competition?

M. Proudhon says, further, that competition is the

opposite of monopoly, that, in consequence, it cannot be the *opposite of association.*

Feudalism was, from its origin, opposed to competition, which did not yet exist. Did it follow that competition was not opposed to feudalism?

In fact, *society, association,* are denominations which may be given to all societies, to feudal society as well as to bourgeois society, which is association based upon competition. How, then, can there be Socialists who, by the single word *association* think to be able to dispose of competition? And how can M. Proudhon himself think to defend competition against Socialism, simply by defining competition by the single word *association?*

All that we have just considered forms the good side of competition, as M. Proudhon understands it. We will now pass on to the evil side, that is to say to the negative side of competition, to its inconveniences, to those qualities in it which are destructive, subversive, maleficent.

The picture of these which M. Proudhon presents to us is a somewhat lugubrious one.

Competition engenders poverty, foments civil war; it "changes the natural zones," confounds nationalities, disturbs families, corrupts the public conscience, "overturns the notions of equity, of justice," of morality, and what is worse, it destroys honest and free commerce and does not even give in exchange *synthetical value,* fixed and honest price. It disenchants everybody, even the economists. It forces things on even to its own destruction.

After all the bad that M. Proudhon says of it, can there be, for the relations of bourgeois society, for its principles and its illusions, an element more disintegrating, more destructive, than competition?

Let us observe that competition always becomes more

THE POVERTY OF PHILOSOPHY

destructive of bourgeois relations in proportion as it exites to a feverish creation of new productive forces—that is to say, of the material conditions of a new society. In this connection, at least, the evil side of competition should have its good.

"Competition, as an economic position or phase, considered in its origin, is the necessary result . . . . of the theory of the reduction of the general cost."

For M. Proudhon, the circulation of the blood must be a consequence of the theory of Harvey.

"*Monopoly* is the fatal term of competition, which the latter engenders by an incessant negation of itself. This generation of monopoly is already the justification of competition . . . . Monopoly is the natural opposite of competition . . . . but from the time that competition is necessary it implies the idea of monopoly, since monopoly is as the seat of each competing individuality."

We rejoice with M. Proudhon that he can for once, at least, properly apply his formula of thesis and antithesis. Everybody knows that modern monopoly is engendered by competition.

As to the content, M. Proudhon devotes himself to some poetic images. Competition makes "of each subdivision of labor a sort of sovereignty in which each individual reposes in his strength and his independence." Monopoly is "the *seat* of each competing individuality." The sovereignty is at least worthy of the seat.

M. Proudhon speaks only of modern monopoly engendered by competition. But we all know that competition was engendered by feudal monopoly. Thus primarily competition has been the contrary of monopoly, and not monopoly the contrary of competition. Therefore modern monopoly is not a simple antithesis; it is, on the contrary, the true synthesis.

THE METAPHYSICS OF POLITICAL ECONOMY

Thesis: Feudal monopoly anterior to competition.
Antithesis: Competition.
Synthesis: Modern monopoly, which is the negation of feudal monopoly in so far as it supposes the *régime* of competition, and which is the negation of competition in so far as it is monopoly.

Thus modern monopoly, bourgeois monopoly, is synthetic monopoly, the negation of the negation, the unity of contraries. It is monopoly in its pure, normal, rational state. M. Proudhon is in contradiction with his own philosophy when he makes of bourgeois monopoly, monopoly in the crude, simple, contradictory, spasmodic state. M. Rossi, whom M. Proudhon often quotes on the subject of monopoly, appears to have more clearly grasped the synthetic character of bourgeois monopoly. In his "Cours d'Économie Politique," he distinguishes between artificial monopolies and natural monopolies. Feudal monopolies, he says, are artificial, that is to say arbitrary; bourgeois monopolies are natural, that is to say rational.

Monopoly is a good thing, reasons M. Proudhon, since it is an economic category, an emanation "from the impersonal reason of humanity." Competition is another good thing since it also is an economic category. But what is not good is the reality of monopoly and the reality of competition. What is worse still is that competition and monopoly devour each other mutually. What is to be done? Seek the synthesis of these two eternal thoughts, drag it from the bosom of God, where it has been deposited from time immemorial.

In practical life we find not only competition, monopoly, and their antagonism, but also their synthesis, which is not a formula but a movement. Monopoly produces competition, competition produces monopoly. The monopolists are made by competition, the competitors become monopolists. If the monopolists restrict competition among themselves by partial association, competition grows among the workers; and the more the mass of the workers grows as against the monopolists of one nation, the more keen becomes the competition between the monopolists of different nations. The synthesis is such that monopoly can only maintain itself by continually passing through the struggle of competition.

In order to dialectically engender the *imposts* which follow *monopoly,* M. Proudhon talks to us of the social genius who, after having intrepidly pursued his zigzag route, "after having marched with a firm step, without regret and without halting, and having *arrived at the angle of monopoly,* casts a melancholy glance backward, and, after profound reflection, fixes imposts on all objects of production, and creates an entire administrative organisation, in order that *all employment should be delivered to the proletariat* and be paid by the men of monopoly."

What is to be said of this genius, who being fasting, walks zigzag? And what is to be said of this promenade which has no other end than to demolish the bourgeoisie by imposts, while these imposts serve precisely to give the bourgeoisie the means of conserving its position as the dominant class?

In order to get a glimpse of the manner in which M. Proudhon treats economic details, it will suffice to say that, according to him, the impost on articles of consumption must have been established with a view to equality and in order to render assistance to the proletariat.

Imposts on articles of consumption have only had their true development since the advent of the bour-

THE METAPHYSICS OF POLITICAL ECONOMY

geoisie. In the hands of industrial capital, that is to say the sober and thrifty wealth which maintained, reproduced, and increased itself by the direct exploitation of labor, the impost on articles of consumption was a means of exploiting the frivolous, joyous, prodigal wealth of the grand lords who did nothing but consume. Sir James Steuart very well explains this primitive object of the impost on articles of consumption in his "Inquiry into the Principles of Political Economy," which he published ten years before Adam Smith.

"Under the pure monarchy," he says, "the prince seems jealous as it were, of growing wealth, and therefore imposes taxes upon people who are growing richer. Under the limited Government they are calculated chiefly to affect those who are growing poorer. Thus the monarch imposes a tax upon industry, where everyone is rated in proportion to the gain *he is supposed* to make by his profession. The poll-tax and *taille,* are likewise proportioned to the *supposed* opulence of everyone liable to them. . . . . In limited Governments, impositions are generally laid upon consumption."

As to the logical succession of imposts, of the balance of commerce, of credit—in the understanding of M. Proudhon—we will merely observe that the English bourgeoisie, having, under William of Orange, attained its political constitution, created at a stroke a new system of taxation, public credit, and the system of protective duties, when it was in a position to freely develop its conditions of existence.

This glimpse will suffice to give the reader a fair idea of the lucubrations of M. Proudhon on police and taxation, the balance of commerce, communism, and population. We defy the most indulgent critic to approach these chapters seriously.

SECTION IV.—PROPERTY AND RENT.

In each historical epoch property is differently developed, and in a series of social relations entirely different. Thus, to define bourgeois property is nothing other than to explain all the social relations of bourgeois production.

To pretend to give a definition of property as of an independent relation, a separate category, an abstract and eternal idea, can only be an illusion of metaphysics or of jurisprudence.

M. Proudhon, while professing to speak of property in general, deals only with property in land, the rent of land.

"The origin of rent, as property, is, so to speak, extra-economic; it exists in certain psychological and moral considerations which are only remotely connected with the production of wealth." (Vol. II., p. 266.)

Thus M. Proudhon recognises his inability to comprehend the economic origin of rent and of property. He acknowledges that this incapacity obliges him to have recourse to psyhcologial and moral considerations, which are indeed only remotely connected with the production of wealth, being closely allied to the exigencies of his historical views. M. Proudhon affirms that in the origin of property there is something mystic and mysterious. But to see mystery in the origin of property, that is to say, to transform the relation of production itself to the distribution of the instruments of production into a mystery, is that not, to use the language of M. Proudhon, to renounce all pretension to economic science?

M. Proudhon is "compelled to recall that at the seventh epoch of economic evolution—credit—the fiction

THE METAPHYSICS OF POLITICAL ECONOMY

having caused the reality to vanish, human activity threatening to lose itself in space, it became necessary *to attach it more closely to nature;* but rent was the price of this new contract."

"The man with forty crowns" represents a Proudhon to come: "My Lord the creator, if you please: each is master in his world; but you will never make me believe that this world where we are is of glass." In such a world, where credit was a means for losing one's self in space, it is quite possible for property to be necessary in order to attach man to nature. In the world of real people, where property in land always precedes credit, the *horror vacui* of M. Proudhon could not exist.

The existence of rent once admitted, whatever may have been its origin, it is contradictorily debated between farmer and landlord. What is the last term of this debate—in other words, what is the mean quota of rent? Here is what M. Proudhon says:

"The theory of Ricardo answers this question. At the beginning of society, when man, newly arrived on earth, had before him only immense forests, when the earth was vast and industry was in its infancy, rent was nil. Land, not yet cultivated by labor, was an object of utility; it was not a value in exchange. It was common, not social. Little by little the multiplication of families and the progress of agriculture caused the price of land to make itself felt. Labor gave its value to the soil: from that sprang rent. The more fruitful a field, with the same quantity of labor, the more it was esteemed; moreover, the tendency of the proprietors was always to attribute to themselves the whole of the fruits of the soil, less the wages of the cultivator, that is to say less the cost of production. Thus property followed in the

THE POVERTY OF PHILOSOPHY

train of labor to take from it all that which, in the product, exeeded the actual cost. Property fulfilled a mystic duty by representing the community face to face with the cultivator. In the design of Providence the cultivator is nothing but a responsible laborer, who must give an account to society of all that he reaps in excess of his legitimate wages. . . . . By essence and destination, therefore, rent is an instrument of distributive justice, one of the thousand means which economic genius puts into operation in order to arrive at equality. It is an immense valuation executed contradictorily by the landlords and farmers, without the possibility of collision, in a superior interest, and the definite result of which must be to equalise the possession of the land between the exploiters of the soil and the industrial community. . . . . It required nothing less than this magic of property to drag from the cultivator the excess of the product which he could not be prevented from regarding as his, and of which he believed himself to be the sole author. Rent, or rather property, broke down agricultural egoism and created a solidarity to which no power, no partition of the land, could have given birth. . . . . At present, the moral effect of property secured, it only remains to distribute the rent."

All this jumble of words may be reduced to this: Ricardo says that the excess of the price of agricultural products over their cost of production, including the ordinary profit and interest of capital, gives the measure of the rent. M. Proudhon does better. He makes the proprietor intervene, as a *deus ex machina*, who drags from the cultivator all the excess of his production over the actual cost of production. He makes use of the intervention of the proprietor, to explain property, of the landlord, to explain rent. He answers the problem by

THE METAPHYSICS OF POLITICAL ECONOMY

restating the same problem and increasing it by a syllable.

We may further observe that in determining rent by the difference of fertility of the soil, M. Proudhon assigns to it a new origin, since land, before being estimated according to the different degrees of fertilty, "was not," according to him, "a value in exchange, but was common." What has it now become, this fiction of rent which sprang from the necessity of attaching to earth man who was likely to lose himself in the infinity of space?

Let us now extricate the doctrine of Ricardo from the providential, allegorical and mystical phrases in which M. Proudhon has been careful to envelop it.

Rent, in the Ricardian sense, is property in land in the bourgeois state—that is to say, feudal property which has been subjected to the conditions of bourgeois production.

We have seen that, according to Ricardo, the price of all products is finally determined by the cost of production including in that industrial profit — in other terms, by the time of labor employed. In the manufacturing industry the price of the product obtained by the minimum of labor regulates the price of all other commodities of the same kind, provided that the least costly and most productive instruments of production may be multiplied to infinity, and that, therefore, free competition necessarily creates a market price—that is to say, a common price—for all the products of the same kind.

In agricultural industry, on the contrary, it is the price of the product obtained by the greatest amount of labor which regulates the price of all the products of the same kind. In the first place, we cannot, as in manufacturing industry, multiply at will the instruments of production of the same degree of productivity—that is to say, the soils of the same degree of fertility. Then, in proportion as population grows, it is necessary to exploit soils of inferior quality, or to expend on the same soil additional capital proportionately less productive than the first. In either case a larger quantity of labor is expended in order to obtain a product proportionally smaller. The needs of the population having rendered this increase of labor necessary, the product of the soil more costly to cultivate has its sale forced as well as that of the more cheaply cultivated soil. Competition levels the market price, and the product of the better soil will fetch as high a price as that of the inferior soil. It is the excess of the price of the products of the superior soil over their cost of production which constitutes rent. If there were always at disposal soils of the same degree of fertility, if, as in manufacturing industry, recourse could always be had to the less costly and more productive machinery, or if the second expenditure of capital produced as much as the first, then the price of agricultural products would be determined by the price of the commodities produced by the better instruments of production, as we have seen in the price of manufactured articles. But also, from this moment, rent would have disappeared.

For the theory of Ricardo to be generally true, it is further necessary that capital could be freely applied to the different branches of industry; that a strongly developed competition between the capitalists should have reduced profits to an equal rate; that the farmer should be no more than an industrial capitalist who asks for the employment of his capital upon the land, a profit equal to that which he would draw from his capital applied to any manufacture; that agricultural exploita-

THE METAPHYSICS OF POLITICAL ECONOMY

tion should be subject to the *régime* of the great industry; in fine, that the landed proprietor himself should aim at nothing more than the monetary revenue.

Rent may no longer exist, as is the case in Ireland, although farming there has been developed to an advanced degree. Rent being the excess, not only over wages, but over the industrial profit, it cannot exist where the revenue of the proprietor is only a previous deduction from wages.

But, far from making of the exploiter of the soil, of the farmer, a simple laborer, and "dragging from the peasant the excess of the product which he cannot be prevented from regarding as his own," rent sets before the landed proprietor the industrial capitalist, instead of the slave, the serf, the tributary, the wage-worker.

Further, a considerable time elapsed before the feudal farmer was replaced by the industrial capitalist. In Germany, for example, this transformation did not begin until the last third of the eighteenth century. It is only in England that this relation between the industrial capialist and the landed proprietor has been fully developed.

So long as there was only the cultivator of M. Proudhon there was no rent. When there is rent the peasant is not the farmer, but the workman, the employé of the farmer. The degradation of the cultivator reduced to the position of simple workman, day-laborer wage-worker, laboring for the industrial capitalist; the intervention of the industrial capitalist, exploiting the land like any other factory; the transformation of the landed proprietor from a petty sovereign into a vulgar usurer: those are the different relations expressed by rent.

Rent, in the Ricardian sense, is patriarchal agricul-

THE POVERTY OF PHILOSOPHY

ture transformed into commercial industry, industrial capital applied to the land, the bourgeoisie of the towns transplanted into the country. Rent, instead of "attaching man to nature," has only attached the exploitation of the land to competition. Once constituted as rent, landed property itself is the result of competition, since thenceforward it depends upon the saleable value of agricultural products. As rent, landed property is mobilised and becomes an effect of commerce. Rent is possible only from the moment in which the development of the industry of the towns and the social organisation resulting therefrom force the landlord to have regard only to venal profit, to the monetary relation of his agricultural products; to see, in fine, in his landed property, only a machine for making money. Rent has so perfectly detached the landed proprietor from the soil, from nature, that he scarcely needs to know his lands, as we see in England. As to the farmer, the industrial capitalist and the agricultural laborer, they are no more attached to the soil which they cultivate than the capitalist and the workman in manufacture are attached to the cotton or the wood they use; they have regard only for the price of their exploitation, for the monetary product. To that fact is due the jeremiads of the reactionary parties who fervently pray for the return of feudalism, for the happy patriarchal life, for the simple and noble manners of our ancestors. The subjection of the soil to the laws which rule every other industry is and will always be the subject of interested condolences. Thus we might say that rent is the motive force which has cast idyllism into the historical movement.

Ricardo, after having supposed bourgeois production as necessary in order to determine rent, applies it nevertheless to landed property in every epoch in every coun-

THE METAPHYSICS OF POLITICAL ECONOMY

try. These are the errors of all economists who regard the conditions of bourgeois production as eternal categories.

From the providential object of rent, which is, for M. Proudhon, the transformation of the cultivator into a responsible workman, he goes on to the equalitarian reward of rent.

Rent, as we have just seen, is constituted by the equal price of the products of lands of *unequal fertility* in such wise that a hectolitre of wheat which has cost 10 francs is sold for 20 francs if the cost of production rises, for an inferior soil, to 20 francs. So long as necessity compels the purchase of all the agricultural products put upon the market, the market price is determined by the highest cost of production. It is, therefore, this equalisation of price, resulting from competition and not from the different fertility of soils, which secures for the proprietor of the superior soil a rent of 10 francs for each hectolitre which his farmer sells.

Let us for a moment suppose that the price of the wheat is determined by the labor-time necessary to produce it, and that in consequence the hectolitre of wheat obtained from the superior soil would be sold at 10 francs, while that obtained from the inferior soil would cost 20. That admitted, the mean market price would be 15 francs; while, according to the law of competition, it is 20 francs. If the mean price was 15 francs there would be nothing for distribution, either equalitarian or other, as there would be no rent. Rent exists only in consequence of the fact that the hectolitre of wheat, which cost the producer 10 francs, is sold for 20 francs. M. Proudhon supposes the equality of the market price, with unequal cost of production, in order

THE POVERTY OF PHILOSOPHY

to arrive at the equalitarian distribution of the product of inequality.

We can understand such economists as Mill, Cherbulliez, Hilditch, and others, demanding that rent should be handed over to the State to be used for the remission of taxation. That is only the frank expression of the hate which the industrial capitalist feels for the landed proprietor, who appears to him as a useless incumbrance, a superfluity in the otherwise harmonious whole of bourgeois production.

But to first take twenty francs for the hectolitre of wheat in order to afterwards make a general distribution of the ten francs too much charged to the consumers, —that would indeed be sufficient to make the social genius pursue its zigzag way in melancholy, ready to knock its head against any corner.

Rent becomes, under the pen of M. Proudhon, "an immense land valuation made independently by the landlords and the farmers in a superior interest, the definite result of which must be to equalise the possession of the land between the exploiters of the soil and the manufacturing classes."

In order for any valuation whatever, determined by rent, to be of practical utility, it is necessary always to remain in the conditions of existing society.

But we have demonstrated that the farm rent, paid by the farmer to the landlord, expresses almost exactly the rent only in those countries most advanced in industry and commerce. Yet this farm rent often includes the interest paid to the landlord for the capital incorporated in the land. The situation of soils, the neighborhood of towns, and very many other circumstances, influence the farm hire and modify the rent. These

THE METAPHYSICS OF POLITICAL ECONOMY

arbitrary reasons will suffice to prove the inexatitude of a land valuation based on rent.

On the other hand rent cannot be a constant indication of the degree of fertility of any land, since the modern application of chemistry constantly changes the nature of the soil, while it is only in recent years that geological knowledge has begun to destroy all the old estimate of relative fertility. It is only about twenty years ago that vast areas in the eastern countries of England were brought into cultivation, they had been left uncultivated for want of appreciating correctly the relations between the nature of the upper soil and of the lower stratum.

Thus history, so far from giving, in rent, a valuation completely formed, simply changes, completely reverses, the valuations already formed.

In fine, fertility is not so much a natural quality as might reasonably be supposed, but is intimately related to existing social conditions. A soil may be very fertile for the raising of corn, yet, nevertheless, the state of the market may induce the cultivator to turn it into an artificial prairie and thus render it barren. M. Proudhon has improvised his valuation, which is not even worth the ordinary valuation, simply in order to give a corporeal form to the *providentially equalitarian object* of rent.

"Rent," continues M. Proudhon, "is the interest paid for a capital which never perishes, namely land. And as this capital is not susceptible of any increase as to its material but only to an indefinite improvement in its use, it results that, while the interest or profit on a loan (*mutuum*) tends to constantly diminish in consequence of the abundance of capital, rent tends to constantly increase by the perfection of the industry from

THE POVERTY OF PHILOSOPHY

which results the improvement in the usages of the soil. ...... Such, in its essence, is rent." (Vol. II., p. 265.)

This time, M. Proudhon sees in rent all the attributes of interest, so far as it arises from a capital of a specific nature. This capital is land, eternal capital, "which is not susceptible of any increase as to its material, but only to an indefinite improvement in its use." In the progressive march of civilisation interest has a constant tendency to fall, while rent constantly tends to rise. Interest falls on account of the abundance of capital; rent rises with the improvements made in industry which have the effect of constantly improving the use of land.

Such is, in its essence, the opinion of M. Proudhon.

Let us begin by examining at what point it is correct to say that rent is the interest on capital.

For the landowner himself rent represents interest on the capital which the land has cost him, or which it would return to him if he sold it. But in buying or selling land, he only buys or sells rent. The price which he has paid in order to acquire the rent is regulated by the general rate of interest and has nothing to do with the nature of rent itself. The interest on capital invested in land is, in general, less than the interest on capital sunk in manufacture or commerce. Thus for him who does not distinguish the interest which land represents to the proprietor from rent itself, the interest on capital in land diminishes much more than the interest on other capitals. But it is not here a question of the price of the sale or purchase of rent, of the saleable value of rent, of capitalized rent, it is a question of rent itself.

The hire of a farm may imply in addition to the rent properly so-called, interest on capital incorporated in the

THE METAPHYSICS OF POLITICAL ECONOMY

land. Then, the proprietor receives this part of the farm hire not as landlord, but as capitalist; that is, however, not the rent, properly speaking, with which we have to deal.

Land, so long as it is not exploited as a means of production, is not capital. Capital in land can be augmented as well as all other means of production. Nothing is added to the material, to speak the language of M. Proudhon, but the soils which serve as instruments of production are multiplied. By merely applying additional capital to land already transformed into means of production land-capital may be augmented without adding anything to the material land, that is to say to the extent of the land. The material land of M. Proudhon has the bounds of the earth for its limits. As to the eternity which he attributes to land we readily grant that, as matter, it has this quality. As capital, land is not more eternal than any other capital.

Gold and silver, which pay interest, are as durable and eternal as land. If the price of gold and silver falls while that of land rises, that is certainly not due to the more or less eternal nature of land.

Land-capital is a fixed capital, but fixed capital is used up as well as circulating capital. The improvements effected in the soil need to be reproduced and maintained; they only last a certain time, a quality which they possess in common with all other improvements of which use is made in order to transform matter into means of production. If land-capital were eternal certain lands would present an entirely different aspect to that which they bear to-day, and we should see the Roman Campagna, Sicily, and Palestine, in all the splendor of their ancient prosperity.

There are, moreover, cases where land-capital may

THE POVERTY OF PHILOSOPHY

disappear, even while the improvements remain incorporated in the land.

In the first place this actually happens every time that rent, properly so-called, is extinguished by the competition of new and more fertile soils; further, the improvements which have a value at a certain period, cease to have that value from the moment that they become universal through the development of agricultural science.

The representative of land-capital is not the landowner but the farmer. The revenue which land gives as capital is industrial interest and profit, and not rent. There are some lands which return this interest and profit, but which pay no rent.

To sum up, land in so far as it gives interest, is land-capital, and, as land-capital, it returns no rent, it does not constitute landed property. Rent results from the social relations in which exploitation is carried on. It cannot result from the nature, more or less fixed, more or less durable, of land. Rent proceeds from society and not from the soil.

According to M. Proudhon "the improvement in the use of land"—a result of "the improvement of industry," is the cause of the constant rise of rent. This improvement, on the contrary, causes it to periodically fall.

In what, in general, does all improvement consist, whether it be in agriculture or in manufacture? It is to produce more with the same amount of labor, it is to produce as much, or even more, with less labor. Thanks to these improvements the farmer can dispense with the employment of a greater quantity of labor for a product proportionally less. He has no need then to have recourse to the inferior soils, and the portions of capital successively applied to the same land are equally productive. Therefore these improvements, so far from causing a constant rise of rent, as M. Proudhon says, are, on the contrary, so many temporary obstacles which oppose its rise.

The English landowners of the seventeenth century were so sensible of this truth that they strenuously opposed all agricultural progress, for fear of seeing their revenues diminish. (See Petty, an English economist of the time of Charles II.)

Section V.—Strikes and the Combination of Workmen.

"Every upward movement in wages can have no other effect than that of a rise in wheat, in wine, &c., that is to say, the effect produced by a dearth. For what are wages? They are the cost price of wheat, &c., the integral price of everything. Let us go further still, wages are the proportion of the elements which compose wealth and which are consumed reproductively each day by the mass of the workers. But, to double wages . . . is to bestow upon each of the producers a part greater than his product, which is contradictory; and if the rise only affects a small number of industries, the result is to provoke a general perturbation in exchanges, in a word, a scarcity . . . . It is impossible, I insist, for the strikes which result in an increase in wages not to lead to a *general dearness*: that is as certain as that two and two make four." (Proudhon, Vol. I., pp. 110 and 111.)

We deny all these assertions, except that two and two make four.

In the first place there is no such thing as *general dearness*. If the price of everything is doubled at the same time as wages, there is no change in prices, there is only a change in terms.

Further, a general rise in wages can never produce a dearness, more or less general, of commodities. In effect, if all industries employed the same number of workmen in proportion to the fixed capital or to the instruments used, a general rise in wages would produce a general reduction of profits, and the current price of commidities would undergo no alteration.

But as the relation of manual labor to fixed capital is not the same in different industries, all the industries which employ relatively a greater mass of fixed capital and less workers will be forced sooner or later to reduce the prices of their commodities. In the contrary case, where the price of their commodities is not reduced, their profit will rise above the common rate of profit. The machines are not wage-workers. Therefore, the general rise in wages will affect those industries less which, compared with the others, employ more machines than workmen. But as competition always tends to level the rate of profits, those which rise above the ordinary rate can only do so temporarily. Thus, apart from some oscillations, a general rise in wages, so far from resulting, as M. Proudhon contends, in a general rise in prices would result in a partial fall, that is to say, a fall in the current price of the commodities which are manufactured chiefly by machinery.

The rise and fall of profit or wages merely expresses the proportion in which the capitalists and the workmen participate in the product of a day of labor without, in most cases, influencing the price of the product. But that "the strikes which are followed by an increase in wages lead to a general rise in prices, to a scarcity even,"

THE METAPHYSICS OF POLITICAL ECONOMY

—these are ideas which could only be hatched in the brain of an unintelligible poet.

In England strikes have regularly given rise to invention and to the application of new machinery. Machines were, we might say, the arms which the capitalists used to defeat revolted labor. The self-acting mule, the greatest invention in modern industry, put the revolted hand-spinners out of action. Even when combination and strikes have no other effect than to arouse against them the efforts of mechanical genius, they always exercise an immense influence on the development of industry.

"I find," continues M. Proudhon, "from an article published by M. Leon Faucher . . . . September, 1845, that for some time English workmen have ceased to form combinations, which is certainly a progress upon which they are to be congratulated. But this improvement in the morality of the workers arises above all from their economic knowledge. 'It is not upon the manufacturers,' cried a working spinner at a meeting at Bolton, 'that wages depend. In periods of depression the masters are only, so to speak, the whips with which necessity is armed, and, whether they will or no, they must strike. The regulating principle is the relation between supply and demand; and the masters have not the power.'" "Well and good," cries M. Proudhon, "these are well developed model workmen, &c., &c. The poverty we have here does not exist in England; it cannot cross the Channel." (Proudhon, Vol. I., pp. 261 and 262.)

Of all the towns in England, Bolton is one in which Radicalism is as fully developed as anywhere. Than the workers of Bolton there are none more revolutionary. During the great agitation in England for the abolition of the Corn Laws, the English manufacturers felt that

THE POVERTY OF PHILOSOPHY

they would be unable to make head against the landowners except by putting the workers in the front of the fight. But, as the interests of the workers were not less opposed to those of the manufacturers than the interests of the manufacturers were opposed to those of the landowners, it was natural to expect that the manufacturers would get the worst of it in the meetings of the workers. But what did the manufacturers do? In order to save appearances they organised meetings composed in great part of foremen and overseers, of the small number of workmen who were devoted to them, and some "friends of commerce," properly so-called. When afterwards the real working people attempted, as at Bolton and Manchester, to take part in such meetings in order to protest against these factitious demonstrations, they were told they were "ticket meetings," to which no one could be admitted without a ticket, and were refused admission. Nevertheless, the placards advertising the meetings had announced them as public demonstrations. Every time these meetings were held the capitalist journals gave glowing accounts, with full and detailed reports of the speeches. It goes without saying that these speeches were made by foremen and overseers. The London newspapers gave literal reproductions of these reports. M. Proudhon is so unfortunate as to take the foremen and overseers for ordinary workmen, and to urge upon them the advice not to cross the Channel.

If in 1844 and in 1845 strikes attracted less attention than formerly, it was because 1844 and 1845 were the two first years of prosperity which English industry had enjoyed since 1837. Nevertheless none of the trade unions were dissolved.

Let us now hear the foremen and overseers of Bolton.

THE METAPHYSICS OF POLITICAL ECONOMY

According to them the manufacturers are not the masters of wages because they are not masters of the price of the product, and they are not masters of the world market. By this argument they gave it to be understood that combinations were not necesary to drag from the masters an increase of wages. M. Proudhon, on the contrary, forbids them to combine for fear that combination may be followed by a rise in wages, which would bring in its train a general scarcity. It is not necessary for us to point out that on one point there is perfect agreement between the foremen and M. Proudhon, that is, that a rise in wages is the equivalent of a rise in the price of products.

But is the fear of a scarcity the true cause of M. Proudhon's ill-will towards combination? No. He cordially agrees with the foremen of Bolton because they determine value by supply and demand, and because they scarcely think of "constituted value," of value passed to the state of constitution, of the constitution of value, comprising the "permanent exchangeability," and all the other "proportionalities of relations" and "relations of proportionalities," flanked by Providence.

"For workers to strike is *illegal*, and it is not only the penal code which says so, it is the economic system, it is the necessity of the established order. . . . That each workman should have the free disposal of his hands and of his person, that can be tolerated, but that workmen should undertake by combination to do violence to monopoly, that is what society can never permit." (Vol. I., pp. 235 and 237.)

M. Proudhon wishes to make an article of the penal code pass for a necessary and general result of bourgeois production.

In England trade combination is permitted by law,

THE POVERTY OF PHILOSOPHY

and it is the economic system which has forced Parliament to give this legal authorisation. In 1825 when, under the minister Huskisson, Parliament had to modify the law in order to bring it more into accord with a state of things resulting from free competition, it was necessary to abolish the laws which prohibited the combination of workmen. The more modern industry and competition develop, the more elements are there which provoke and support competition, and as soon as combinations have become an economic fact, acquiring greater consistency day by day, they will not be slow in becoming a legal fact.

Thus the article of the penal code only proves at most that modern industry and competition were not sufficiently developed, under the Constituent Assembly and under the Empire, for the legal recognition of combination.

The economists and the Socialists are agreed on one point. That is, in condemning combinations. Only they have different motives for their act of condemnation.

The economists say to the workers: Do not combine. By combining you hinder the steady progress of industry, you prevent the manufacturers from executing their orders, you disturb commerce and precipitate the introduction of machinery which, by rendering your labor in part useless, forces you to accept still lower wages. Otherwise you may do very well, your wages will be always determined by the relations between the demand for and the supply of hands, and it is an effort as ridiculous as dangerous to revolt against the eternal laws of political economy.

The Socialists say to the workers: Do not combine, because at the end of the account what will you have gained by it? An increase of wages? The economists

THE METAPHYSICS OF POLITICAL ECONOMY

prove to demonstration that the few pence which you temporarily gain if you succeed, will be followed by a lasting reduction. Clever statisticians prove to you that it will take you years to recover by the rise in wages the expenditure you have had to make in order to organise and maintain your combination. And we—we, as Socialists tell you, that apart from this question of money, you will be not less workmen, and the masters will be always the masters as before. Therefore, no combinations, no politics; for after all, to form combinations is that not having to do with politics?

The economists desire that the workers should remain in society as it is formed, and as they have recorded and ratified it in their manuals.

The Socialists desire the workers to leave the old society in order to be the better able to enter into the new society which they have prepared with so much foresight.

In spite of the one and the other, in spite of the manuals and the utopias, combinations have not ceased to progress and to grow with the development and growth of modern industry. It is at such a point now that the degree of development of combination in a country marks clearly the degree which that country occupies in the hierarchy of the world market. In England, where industry has attained the highest degree of development, the combinations are the largest and best organised.

In England these combinations are not confined to a partial organisation with no other object than a temporary strike, and which will disappear when that is over. Permanent combinations have been formed—trade unions—which serve as a rampart for the workers in their struggle with the capitalists. And at the present time all these local trade unions have a centre or

THE POVERTY OF PHILOSOPHY

union in the "National Association of United Trades, the central committee of which is in London,.and which already numbers 80,000 members.

The organisation of strikes, combinations, trade unions, marches simultaneously with the political struggles of the workers, who now constitute a great political party under the name of Chartists.

It is under the form of these combinations that the first attempts at association among themselves have always been made by the workers.

The great industry masses together in a single place a crowd of people unknown to each other. Competition divides their interests. But the maintenance of their wages, this common interest which they have against their employer, unites them in the same idea of resistance —combination. Thus combination has always a double end, that of eliminating competition among themselves while enabling them to make a general competition against the capitalist. If the first object of resistance has been merely to maintain wages, in proportion as the capitalists in their turn have combined with the idea of repression, the combinations, at first isolated, have formed in groups, and, in face of constantly united capital, the maintenance of the association became more important and necessary for them than the maintenance of wages. This is so true that the English economists are all astonished at seeing the workers sacrifice a good part of their wages on behalf of the associations which, in the eyes of these economists, were only established in support of wages. In this struggle—a veritable civil war—are united and developed all the elements necessary for a future battle. Once arrived at that point, association takes a political character.

The economic conditions have in the first place trans-

THE METAPHYSICS OF POLITICAL ECONOMY

formed the mass of the people of a country into wage-workers. The dominaiton of capital has created for this mass of people a common situation with common interests. Thus this mass is already a class, as opposed to capital, but not yet for itself. In the struggle, of which we have only noted some phases, this mass unites, it is constituted as a class for itself. The interests which it defends are the interests of its class. But the struggle between class and class is a political struggle.

In the bourgeoisie we have two phases to distinguish, that during which it is constituted as a class under the *régime* of feudalism and absolute monarchy, and that wherein, already constituted as a class, it overthrew feudalism and monarchy in order to make of society a bourgeois society. The first of these phases was the longest and necessitated the greatest efforts. That also commenced with partial combinations against the feudal lords.

Many researches have been made to trace the different historical phases through which the bourgeoisie has passed from the early commune to its constitution as a class.

But when it becomes a question of rendering an account of the strikes, combinations, and other forms in which before our eyes the proletarians effect their organisation as a class, some are seized with fear while others express a transcendental disdain.

An oppressed class is the vital condition of every society based upon the antagonism of classes. The emancipation of the oppressed class therefore necessarily implies the creation of a new society. In order for the oppressed class to be emancipated it is necessary that the productive powers already acquired and the existing social relations should no longer be able to exist side by

THE POVERTY OF PHILOSOPHY

side. Of all the instruments of production the greatest productive power is the revolutionary class itself. The organisation of the revolutionary elements as a class supposes the existence of all the productive forces which can be engendered in the bosom of the old society.

Is that to say that after the fall of the old society there will be a new class domination, comprised in a new political power? No.

The essential condition of the emancipation of the working class is the abolition of all classes, as the condition of the emancipation of the third estate of the bourgeois order, was the abolition of all estates, all orders.

The working class will substitute, in the course of its development, for the old order of civil society an association which will exclude classes and their antagonism, and there will no longer be political power, properly speaking, since political power is simply the official form of the antagonism in civil society.

In the meantime, the antagonism between the proletariat and the bourgeoisie is a struggle between class and class, a struggle which, carried to its highest expression, is a complete revolution. Would it, moreover, be matter for astonishment if a society, based upon the *antagonism* of classes, should lead ultimately to a brutal *conflict,* to a hand-to-hand struggle as its final *dénoument?*

Do not say that the social movement excludes the political movement. There has never been a political movement which was not at the same time social.

It is only in an order of things in which there will be no longer classes or class antagonism that *social evolutions* will cease to be *political revolutions*. Until then, on

THE METAPHYSICS OF POLITICAL ECONOMY

the eve of each general reconstruction of society, the last word of social science will ever be:—

"Le combat ou la mort; la lutte sanguinaire ou le néant. C'est ainsi que la question est invinciblement posée."*

GEORGE SAND.

Finis.

* Combat or death; bloody struggle or extinction. It is thus that the question is irresistibly put.

APPENDIX I.

PROUDHON JUDGED BY KARL MARX.*

London, January 24, 1865.

Sir,

You ask me for a detailed criticism of the works of Proudhon. I regret that I have not the time to comply with your request. Moreover, I have none of his writings at hand. However, as proof of my goodwill I send you these few hasty notes.

I do not remember the first essays of Proudhon. His schoolboy work on "A Universal Language" shows with what recklessness he grappled with problems for the solution of which he lacked the most elementary knowledge.

His first work: "What is Property?" is very much his best. It was an epoch-making book, if not from the novelty of what he said, at least by the freshness and boldness of his manner of putting everything. The French Socialists, with whose writings he was ac-

---

* Extract from the *Sozial-Democrat*, Nos. 16, 17 and 18 January, 1865.

APPENDIX

quainted, had naturally not only criticised property from different points of view, but had, in utopian fashion, suppressed it. In his book Proudhon is to Saint Simon and Fourier almost what Feuerbach is to Hegel. Compared with Hegel, Feuerbach is very poor. Nevertheless, *after* Hegel, he made an epoch, because he accentuated certain points, disagreeable for the Christian conscience and important for philosophic progress, but which had been left by Hegel in an obscure and mystic light.

The style of this writing of Proudhon is, if I may say so, bold and vigorous, and it is its style, in my opinion, which is its great merit. We see that even when he merely reproduces he discovers; that what he says is new to him, and that it serves him as something new.

The provoking audacity with which he lays hands on the economic sanctuary, the brilliant paradoxes by which he ridicules the dull bourgeois common-sense, his incisive criticism, his bitter irony, with here and there a profound and sincere sentiment of revolt against the established order of things, his revolutionary spirit—this it is which electrifies the readers of "What is Property?" and made the book on its appearance a powerful revolutionary impulse. In a rigorously scientific history of political economy, the work would scarcely be worthy of mention. But these sensational books play a part in the sciences as well as in literature. Take, for example, Malthus's "Essay on Population." The first edition was simply a sensational pamphlet, and a plagiarism from one end to the other into the bargain. Yet what an impression has this pasquinade produced on humanity?

If I had before me this book of Proudhon's it would be easy for me to give some illustrations of his first style. In the chapters which he himself considers the best he imitates the contradictory method of Kant, the only

APPENDIX

German philosopher that he knew at that time, from translation, and he leaves a strong impression that for him, as for Kant, the solution of these contradictions is "beyond" the human understanding, that is to say, that his understanding is incapable of solving them.

But in spite of its alluring iconoclasticism, there is to be found, even in this first work, this contradiction that Proudhon, on one hand, deals with society from the point of view of the petty peasant (later of the petty bourgeois) of France, and on the other he applies the standard which the Socialists have transmitted to him.

Beyond that the very title of the book indicates its insufficiency. The question was too baldly put for it to be answered correctly. Græco-Roman property was replaced by feudal property, and that by bourgeois property. History itself conveys the criticism of the condition of property in the past. The question with which Proudhon had to deal was as to the relations of modern bourgeois property. To the question what were these relations, one could only reply by a critical analysis of political economy, embracing the whole of the relations of property, not in their juridical expression as relations of will, but in their real form as relation of material production. As Proudhon subordinated the whole of these economic relations to the juridical notion of property, he could not go beyond the response which had been already given by Brissot before 1789 and in the same terms: "Property is Robbery."*

The conclusion to be drawn from all this is that the juridical notions of the bourgeoisie on *robbery* apply as well to its *honest* profits. On the other hand, as robbery,

---

* Brissot de Warville, "Recherches sur le droit de propriété et sur le vol," &c. Berlin 1782. (In the sixth volume of the "Bibliothèque du législateur," by Brissot de Warville.)

APPENDIX

being a violation of property, presupposes property, Proudhon embroils himself in all kinds of confused and fantastic notions with regard to *true* bourgeois property.

During my stay in Paris, in 1844, I had personal relations with Proudhon. I recall this circumstance, because up to a certain point I am responsible for his "sophistication," a word which the English use for the adulteration of a commodity. In our long discussions—often lasting all through the night—I infected him with Hegelianism, to his great prejudice, since, not knowing German, he could not study the matter thoroughly. What I had begun, M. Karl Grün, after my expulsion from France, continued. But this professor of German philosophy had the further advantage over me of understanding nothing of what he taught.

A short time before the publication of his second important work, "Philosophie de la Misère," &c., Proudhon informed me of it in a long and detailed letter, in which among other things he said: "I await the blow of your critical rod." And very soon this fell upon him (in my "Misère de la Philosophie") in such a fashion as to for ever shatter our friendship.

From the foregoing you can see that the "Philosophie de la Misère, ou Système des Contradictions Economiques," ought, in short, to give the answer to the question: "What is property?" As a matter of fact, Proudhon did not begin his economic studies until after the publication of this first book; he then discovered that in order to solve the question he had put, it was necessary to reply, not by invective, but by an analysis of modern political economy. At the same time he endeavored to establish the system of "economic categories" by means of dialectic. Hegelian contradiction had to re-

APPENDIX

place the insoluble contradiction of Kant as a means of development.

For a criticism of these two large volumes I must refer you to my reply. I have there, among other things, shown how slightly Proudhon has penetrated the mystery of scientific dialectic, and how far, on the other hand, he shares the illusions of "speculative" philosophy. Instead of regarding the economic categories as the theoretical expressions of the historical relations of production, corresponding to a given degree of the development of material production, his imagination transforms them into "eternal ideas," existing before any reality, and in this manner he arrives, in a round-about way, at the point from which he started, the point of view of bourgeois economy.*

Then I show how defective and rudimentary is his knowledge of political economy, of which nevertheless, he undertakes the criticism, and how, with the utopians, he sets himself to seek for a pretended "science" which may furnish him with a ready-made formula for "the solution of the social question," instead of drawing his science from critical knowledge of the historical movement, the movement which must itself produce the material conditions of social emancipation. What I, above all, denounce, is that M. Proudhon has only imperfect ideas, confused and false with regard to the basis of all political economy—exchange-value—a circum-

---

* In saying that existing conditions—the conditions of bourgeois production—are natural, the economists give it to be understood that these are the relations in which wealth is created and the productive forces are developed conformably to the laws of nature. Thus these relations are themselves natural laws, independent of the influence of time. They are eternal laws which must always govern society. Thus there has been history, but there is no longer any.

APPENDIX

stance which leads him to see the foundation of a new science in a utopian interpretation of the theory of Ricardo. Finally, I sum up my judgment of his point of view in these words:—

Each economic relation has a good and bad side: that is the single point upon which M. Proudhon does not contradict himself. The good side, he sees explained by the economists; the bad side, he sees denounced by the Socialists. He borrows from the economists the necessity of eternal relations; he borrows from the Socialists the illusion of seeing in poverty only poverty. He is in agreement with both in wishing to refer it to the authority of science. Science, for him, is reduced to the insignificant proportions of a scientific formula. It is thus that M. Proudhon flatters himself to have made the criticism of both political economy and of communism: he is below both the one and the other. Below the economists, since as a philosopher, who has under his hand a magic formula, he has believed himself able to do without entering into purely economic details; below the Socialists, since he has neither sufficient courage nor sufficient intelligence to raise himself, were it only speculatively, above the bourgeois horizon.

He wished to soar as man of science above the bourgeoisie and the proletarians; he is only the petty bourgeois, tossed about constantly between capital and labor, between political economy and communism.

However severe this judgment may appear, I am obliged still to maintain it word for word. But it is important to remember that at the time when I declared and proved theoretically that Proudhon's book was only the code of petty bourgeois Socialism, this same Proudhon was being anathematised as an arch-revolutionist by the economists and the Socialists of the period. That is

APPENDIX

the reason why I did not at a later period raise my voice with those who cried out about his "betrayal" of the revolution. It was not his fault if, at first ill-understood by others as well as by himself, he has not fulfilled the hopes which nothing had ever justified.

The "Philosophie de la Misère," as compared with "Qu'est-ce que la Propriété?" displays very unfavorably all the defects of Proudhon's manner of exposition. The style is often what the French call bombastic. A pretentious and "speculative" piece of fustian, which, represented as German philosophy, presents itself everywhere where Gallic perspicacity is at fault. That which he trumpets in your ears, with the voice of a blustering buffoon, is his own glorification, wearisome nonsense and eternal rodomontade about his pretended "science." Instead of the true and natural warmth which illumines his first book, in this Proudhon declaims systematically and fails to excite any feeling. Add to this the awkward and disagreeable didactic pedantry, which serves for erudition, of the man who has lost his former pride of being an independent and original thinker, and who now, as a parvenu of science, thinks he should swagger and boast of what he is not and of what he does not possess. After that his sentiments of a tallow chandler, which lead him to attack in a most unseemly and brutal manner—but which is neither discerning, nor profound, nor even just —a man like Cabet, who was always worthy of respect because of his political *rôle* in the midst of the proletariat, while he does the amiable towards a Dunnoyer (a Councillor of State, it is true) who has no importance beyond that of having preached, with a comical seriousness, throughout the whole of three great volumes, insupportably tiresome, a hypercriticism thus described by

APPENDIX

Helvetius: "We desire that the unfortunate should be perfect."

In fact, the revolution of February happened very unfortunately for Proudhon, who, a few weeks previously, had proved definitely and irrefutably that the "era of revolutions" was past for ever. Nevertheless his attitude in the National Assembly merits nothing but praise, although it proved his lack of intelligence of the situation. After the insurrection of June this attitude was an act of great courage. It had further this happy result, that M. Thiers, in his reply to the propositions of Proudhon, which was afterwards published as a book, revealed the mean, petty pedestal upon which the intellectual pillar of the French bourgeoisie was raised. Compared with Thiers, Proudhon assumed the proportions of an ancient colossus.

The last economic acts and achievements of Proudhon were his discovery of "Free Credit," and of the "People's Bank" which should realise it. In my work "Zur Kritik der Politischen Œkonomie" ("Criticism of Political Economy"), Berlin, 1859 (pp. 59-64), you will find the proof that these Proudhonian ideas are based upon a complete ignorance of the first elements of bourgeois political economy—the relation between commodity and money—while their practical realisation was nothing but the reproduction of better elaborated projects of a much earlier period. There is no doubt, there is indeed evidence to show, that the development of credit, which has served in England in the beginning of the eighteenth century, and more recently in this, to transfer wealth from one class to another, might also serve, in certain political and economic conditions, to accelerate the emancipation of the working class. But to consider interest-bearing capital as the principal form of capital,

APPENDIX

and to wish to make of a particular application of credit—the pretended abolition of the rate of interest—to think to make that the basis of the social transformation—that was indeed a petty chandler's fantasy. Moreover, we find that had been already elaborated *con amore* among the spokesmen of the small shopkeeping class of England in the seventeenth century. The polemic of Proudhon against Bastiat with reference to interest-bearing capital (1850) is far below his "Philosophie de la Misère." He succeeds in allowing himself to be beaten even by Bastiat, and cries and blusters every time that his adversary deals him a blow.

Some years ago Proudhon wrote a thesis on imposts, published in opposition to my theories by the Government of the Canton of Vaud. In that work was extinguished the last ray of genius; nothing of him remains but the petty bourgeois pure and simple.

The political and philosophical writings of Proudhon have all the same dual and contradictory character which we have found in his economic work. Besides, they have only a local importance, limited to France. His attacks upon the religion and the Church had always a great local value in a period when the French Socialists boasted of their religious sentiments as of something superior to the Voltairianism of the eighteenth century and the German atheism af the nineteenth. If Peter the Great overthrew Russian barbarism by barbarity, Proudhon did his best to overthrow French commonplace by commonplaces.

The works which cannot be regarded merely as bad writings, but are simply vile trash, which, however, were quite in keeping with the petty chandler sentiment—were, his book on the *Coup d'Etat,* in which he coquets with Louis Bonaparte, and endeavors to make him acceptable

APPENDIX

to the French workmen, and that against Poland, which, in honor of the Czar, he treats with the cynicism of an idiot.

Proudhon has often been compared to Jean Jacques Rousseau. Nothing could be more erroneous. He resembles rather Nicolas Linguet, whose "Theorie des Lois Civiles" is, moreover, a work of genius.

The nature of Proudhon leads him to dialectics. But having never comprehended scientific dialectic, he gets no further than sophistry. In fact, that arises from his petty bourgeois point of view. The petty bourgeois, precisely like our own historian Raumer, always speaks of one side and of the other side. Two opposing, contradictory currents dominate his material interests, and in consequence his religious, scientific and artistic views, his morality, and in fact his whole being. If he is besides, like Proudhon, a man of intellect, he will very soon be able to juggle with his own contradictions and to elaborate them in striking, noisy, if sometimes brilliant, paradoxes. Scientific charlatanism and political compromises are inseparable from such a point of view. There is, in such case, only a single motive, individual vanity, and as with all vain people, there is no question of anything beyond the mere effect of the moment, the success of the hour. In this is necessarily lost the simple moral tact which would preserve a Rousseau, for example, from all compromise, even apparent, with the powers that be.

Perhaps posterity will say, to distinguish this most recent phase of French history, that Louis Bonaparte was its Napoleon, and Proudhon its Rousseau-Voltaire.

Yours, &c.,

KARL MARX.

APPENDIX II.*

The theory of labor time as the unity of direct measure of money was developed in a systematic manner for the first time by John Gray.†

A central national bank, by the aid of its branches, would certify the time employed in the production of the different commodities. In exchange for his commodity the producer would receive an official certificate of its value—that is to say, a receipt for the labor time contained in his commodity,** and these notes of a week of

---

* (Extract from Marx's work "Zur Kritik der Politischen Œkonomie," Berlin, 1859, pp. 61-64.)

† John Gray.—"The Social System, &c.: Treatise on the Principle of Exchange," Edinburgh, 1831. Composed by the same author: "Lectures on the Nature and Use of Money," Edinburgh, 1848. After the revolution of February, Gray sent to the Provisional Government a memorial in which he informed them that it was not the "organisation of labor" which France needed, but an "organisation of exchange," a completely elaborated plan of which was to be found in the system of money which he had discovered. The worthy John never imagined that sixteen years after the publication of his "Social System," a patent would be taken out for the same discovery by Proudhon, that genius so fertile in invention.

** Gray.—"The Social System," &c., p. 63. "Money should be merely a receipt, an evidence that the holder of it has either contributed certain value to the national stock of wealth, or that he has acquired a right to the same value from someone who has contributed to it."

APPENDIX

labor, a day of labor, an hour of labor, would represent the equivalent which the holder could receive of any other commodities which were in the stores of the bank.* That is the fundamental principle which he has carefully developed in all its details, based upon existing English institutions. With this system, says Gray, "it would be as easy to sell for money as it is now to buy with money; production would be the uniform and inexhaustible source of the demand."† The precious metals would lose the "privilege" which they have over other commodities, and "would take the place which belongs to them on the market side by side with butter, eggs, cloth, and calico; and their value would interest us no more than that of diamonds."** Ought we to retain our artificial measure of value, gold, and fetter thus the productive forces of the country, or ought we not rather to make use of the natural measure of value, labor, and liberate the productive forces?*** Since labor time is the actual measure of value, why by the side of it should there be another, extrinsic, value? Why should exchange-value be transformed into price? Why do all commodities estimate their value in a single commodity, money, which thus becomes equal to the value of exchange?

That was the problem which Gray had to solve. Instead of solving it, he imagines that commodities can

---

* "An estimated value being previously put upon produce, let it be lodged in a bank, and drawn out again, whenever it is required, merely stipulating, by common consent, that he who lodges any kind of property in the proposed national bank may take out of it an equal value of whatever it may contain, instead of being obliged to draw out the self-same thing that he put in."—*Ibid*, p. 68.

† *Ibid*, p. 16.

** Gray.—"Lectures on Money," &c., p. 180.

*** Ibid, p. 169.

APPENDIX

assort themselves, in direct relation with each other, as the products of social labor. But they cannot assort themselves in relation to each other otherwise than as they are. Commodities are the immediate products of individual labors, independent and isolated, which can express themselves as general social labor only by changing themselves in the process of individual exchange; labor, in the production of commodities, only becomes social labor by losing its character of individual labor. In representing the labor time contained in commodities as labor time directly social, Gray represents it as collective labor or as the labor time of individuals directly associated. In such conditions, as a matter of fact, a specific commodity, such as gold or silver, could not be for the other commodities the incarnation of labor in general, value in exchange would not become price, but neither would use-value become value in exchange, the product would not become a commodity, and thus would disappear the basis upon which bourgeois production rests. But that is not the idea of Gray. The products must be produced as commodities, but they must not be exchanged as commodities.

Gray confides to a National Bank the execution of this pious desire. On one side society, by the intermediary of the National Bank, renders the individuals independent of the conditions of individual exchange, and on the other side it leaves them to continue to produce on the basis of individual exchange. Logic compels Gray to successively deny all the conditions of bourgeois production, although he desires merely to "reform" money, the consequence of the exchange of commodities. He transforms capital into national capital,[1] property in

---

[1] The business of every country ought to be conducted on a national capital.— John Gray, "The Social System," p. 71.

APPENDIX

land, into national land,* and when we look more closely into it we see that he does not receive in one hand the commodities and deliver with the other certificates for labor received, but that he regulates production itself. In his last work, "Lectures on Money," in which Gray sets himself to present his labor-money as a purely bourgeois reform, he loses himself in still more transparent absurdities.

Every commodity is money, that is Gray's theory, and this is the result of his incomplete and, therefore, mistaken analysis of commodities. The "organic" construction of "labor-money," of the "national bank," and the stores of commodities," is only a dream in which we are enabled to get a glimpse of the dogma as a universal law. The dogma that a commodity is money, or that the labor of an individual contained in it is social labor, does not become a truth simply because a bank believes in it and acts upon it. Failure in this case plays the part of practical criticism. What Gray has not said, and what he has not imagined—that is to say, that labor-money is an alluring economic phrase for those who have a pious desire to dispense with the use of money, with the value of exchange of commodities, with the commodities of bourgeois society—has been loudly proclaimed by English Socialists who have written before and since himself.†

But it was reserved for Proudhon and his school to seriously proclaim the degradation of money and the exaltation of commodities, as the principle of Socialism,

---

* The land to be transformed into national property.—*Ibid*, p. 298.

† For instance, B. W. Thompson's "An Enquiry into the Distribution of wealth, &c.," London, 1827. Bray:"Labor's Wrongs and Labor's Remedy," Leeds, 1839.

APPENDIX

and therefore to reduce Socialism to an elementary misconception of the necessary dependence which exists between commodity and money.*

---

* As a compendium of this melodramatic theory of money may be cited the work of M. Alfred Darimon, "De la Réforme des Banques," Paris, 1856.

APPENDIX III.

(1.) — FREE TRADE.[1]

A Speech Delivered before the Democratic Association of Brussels, at its Public Meeting, January 9, 1848. By Karl Marx.

Gentlemen,— The Repeal of the Corn Laws in England is the greatest triumph of Free Trade in the nineteenth century. In every country where manufacturers speak of Free Trade, they have in mind chiefly Free Trade in corn or raw material generally. To burden foreign corn with protective duties is infamous, it is to speculate on the hunger of the people.

---

[1] The speech on free exchange, by Marx, is reproduced textually from the original pamphlet published in Brussels in 1848, and which has become so rare that we know of no other copy than that of Engels, from which the German, English, Italian, and Russian translations, which appeared later, have been made. [Note by the editor of the French edition, 1896.]

APPENDIX

Cheap food, high wages, for this alone the English Free Traders have spent millions, and their enthusiasm has already infected their continental brethren. And, generally speaking, all those who advocate Free Trade do so in the interests of the working class.

But, strange to say, the people for whom cheap food is to be procured at all costs are very ungrateful. Cheap food has as bad a repute in England as cheap government has in France. The people see in these self-sacrificing gentlemen, in Bowring, Bright and Co., their worst enemies and the most shameless hypocrites.

Everyone knows that in England the struggle between Liberals and Democrats takes the name of the struggle between Free Traders and Chartists. Let us see how the English Free Traders have proved to the people the good intentions that animate them.

This is what they said to the factory hands —

" The duty on corn is a tax upon wages; this tax you pay to the landlords, those mediæval aristocrats; if your position is a wretched one, it is so only on account of the high price of the most indispensable articles of food."

The workers in turn asked of the manufacturers,—

" How is it that in the course of the last thirty years while our commerce and manufacture has immensely increased, our wages have fallen far more rapidly, in proportion, than the price of corn has gone up?

" The tax which you say we pay the landlords is scarcely threepence a week per worker. And yet the wages of the hand-loom weaver fell, between 1815 and 1843, from 28s. per week to 5s., and the wages of the power-loom weavers, between 1823 and 1843, from 20s. per week to 8s.

" And during the whole of the time that portion of the tax which you say we pay the landlord has never

APPENDIX

exceeded threepence. And, then, in the year 1834, when tell us? You said, 'If you are poor, it is only because you tell us? You said,'If you are poor, it is only because you have too many children, and your marriages are more productive than your labor!'

"These are the very words you spoke to us, and you set about making new Poor Laws, and building workhouses, those bastilles of the proletariat."

To this manufacturers replied,—

"You are right, worthy laborers: it is not the price of corn alone, but competition of the hands among themselves as well, which determines wages.

"But just bear in mind the circumstance that our soil consists of nothing but rocks and sandbanks. You surely do not imagine that corn can be grown in flowerpots! Therefore, if, instead of wasting our labor and capital upon a thoroughly sterile soil, we were to give up agriculture, and devote ourselves exclusively to commerce and manufacture, all Europe would abandon its factories, and England would form one huge factory town, with the whole of the rest of Europe for its agricultural districts."

While thus haranguing his own workingmen, the manufacturer is interrogated by the small tradesmen, who exclaim,—

"If we repeal the Corn Laws, we shall indeed ruin agriculture; but, for all that, we shall not compel other nations to give up their own factories, and buy our goods. What will the consequences be? I lose my customers in the country, and the home market is destroyed."

The manufacturer turns his back upon the workingmen and replies to the shopkeeper,—

"As to that, you leave it to us! Once rid of the duty

APPENDIX

on corn, we shall import cheaper corn from abroad. Then we shall reduce wages at the very time when they are rising in the countries where we get our corn. Thus in addition to the advantages which we already enjoy we shall have lower wages, and with all these advantages, we shall easily force the Continent to buy of us."

But now the farmers and agricultural laborers join in the discussion.

"And what, pray, is to become of us? Are we to help in passing a sentence of death upon agriculture, when we get our living by it? Are we to let the soil be torn from beneath our feet?"

For all answer the Anti-Corn Law League contented itself with offering prizes for the three best essays upon the wholesome influence of the Repeal of the Corn Laws on English agriculture.

These prizes were carried off by Messrs. Hope, Morse, and Greg, whose essays were distributed by thousands throughout the agricultural districts. One of the prize essayists devotes himself to proving that neither the tenant farmer nor the agricultural laborer would lose by the repeal of the Corn Laws, and that the landlord alone would lose.

"The English tenant farmer," he exclaims, "need not fear repeal, because no other country can produce such good corn so cheaply as England. Thus, even if the price of corn fell, it would not hurt you, because this fall would only affect rent, which would go down, while the profit of capital and the wages of labor would remain stationary."

The second prize essayist, Mr. Morse, maintains, on the contrary, that the price of corn will rise in consequence of repeal. He is at infinite pains to prove that protective

APPENDIX

duties have never been able to secure a remunerative price for corn.

In support of his assertion he quotes the fact that, wherever foreign corn has been imported, the price of corn in England has gone up considerably, and that when little corn has been imported the price has fallen greatly. This prize-winner forgets that the importation was not the cause of the high price, but that the high price was the cause of the importation. In direct contradiction of his colleague, he asserts that every rise in the price of corn is profitable to both the tenant farmer and laborer, but does not benefit the landlord.

The third prize essayist, Mr. Greg, who is a large manufacturer and whose work is addressed to the large tenant farmers, could not afford to echo such silly stuff. His language is more scientific.

He admits that the Corn Laws can increase rent only by increasing the price of corn, and that they can raise the price of corn only by inducing the investment of capital upon land of inferior quality, and this is a perfectly natural explanation.

In proportion as population increases, it inevitably follows, if foreign corn cannot be imported, that less fruitful soil must be called into requisition, the cultivation of which involves more expense and the product of which is consequently dearer. There being a demand for all the corn thus produced, it will all be sold. The price for all of it will of necessity be determined by the price of the product of the inferior soil. The difference between this price and the cost of production upon soil of better quality constitutes the rent paid for the use of the better soil.

If, therefore, in consequence of the repeal of the Corn Laws, the price of corn falls, and if, as a matter of

APPENDIX

course, rent falls with it, it is because inferior soil will no longer be cultivated. Thus the reduction of rent must inevitably ruin a number of the tenant farmers.

These remarks are necessary in order to make Mr. Greg's language comprehensible.

"The small farmers," he says, "who cannot support themselves by agriculture must take refuge in manufacture. As to the large tenant farmers, they cannot fail to profit by the arrangement; either the landlord will be obliged to sell them their land very cheap, or leases will be made out for very long periods. This will enable tenant farmers to invest more capital in their farms, to use agricultural machinery on a larger scale, and to save manual labor, which will, moreover, be cheaper, on account of the general fall in wages, the immediate consequence of the repeal of the Corn Laws."

Dr. Bowring conferred upon all these arguments the consecration of religion, by exclaiming at a public meeting, "Jesus Christ is Free Trade, and Free Trade is Jesus Christ."

It may be easily understood that all this cant was not calculated to make cheap bread tasteful to workingmen.

Besides, how should the workingmen understand the sudden philanthropy of the manufacturers, the very men who were still busy fighting against the Ten Hours Bill, which was to reduce the working day of the mill hands from twelve hours to ten?

To give you an idea of the philanthropy of these manufacturers I would remind you of the factory regulations in force in all their mills.

Every manufacturer has for his own special use a regular penal code by means of which fines are inflicted for every voluntary or involuntary offence. For instance, the operative pays so much when he has the misfortune

APPENDIX

to sit down on a chair, or whisper, or speak, or laugh; if he is a few moments late; if any part of a machine breaks, or if he turns out work of an inferior quality, &c. The fines are always greater than the damage really done by the workman. And to give the workingman every opportunity for incurring fines the factory clock is set forward, and he is given bad material to make into good stuff. An overseer unskilful in multiplying infractions of rules is soon discharged.

You see gentlemen, this private legislation is enacted for the especial purpose of creating such infractions, and infractions are manufactured for the purpose of making money. Thus the manufacturer uses every means of reducing the nominal wage, and even profiting by accidents over which the workers have no control.

And these manufacturers are the same philanthropists who have tried to persuade the workers that they were capable of going to immense expense for the sole and express purpose of improving the condition of those same workingmen! On the one hand they nibble at the workers' wages in the meanest way by means of factory regulations, and, on the other, they are prepared to make the greatest sacrifices to raise those wages by means of the Anti-Corn Law League.

They build great palaces, at immense expense, in which the league takes up its official residence. They send an army of missionaries to all corners of England to preach the gospel of Free Trade; they print and distribute gratis thousands of pamphlets to enlighten the workingman upon his own interests. They spend enormous sums to buy over the press to their side. They organise a vast administrative system for the conduct of the Free Trade movement, and bestow all the wealth of their eloquence

APPENDIX

upon public meetings. It was at one of these meetings that a workingman exclaimed boldly,—

"If the landlords were to sell our bones, you manufacturers would be the first to buy them, and to put them through the mill and make flour of them."

The English workingmen have appreciated to the fullest extent the significance of the struggle between the lords of the land and of capital. They know very well that the price of bread was to be reduced in order to reduce wages, and that the profit of capital would rise in proportion as rent fell.

Ricardo, the apostle of the English Free Traders, the leading economist of our century, entirely agrees with the workers upon this point.

In his celebrated work upon Political Economy he says: "If instead of growing our own corn..... we discover a new market from which we can supply ourselves .... at a cheaper price, wages will fall and profits rise. The fall in the price of agricultural produce reduces the wages, not only of the laborer employed in cultivating the soil, but also of all those employed in commerce or manufacture."

And do not believe, gentlemen, that it is a matter of indifference to the workingman whether he receives only four francs on account of corn being cheaper, when he had been receiving five francs before.

Have not his wages always fallen in comparison with profit? And is it not clear that his social position has grown worse as compared with that of the capitalist? Beside which he loses actually. So long as the price of corn was higher and wages were also higher, a small saving in the consumption of bread sufficed to procure him other enjoyments. But as soon as bread is cheap,

APPENDIX

and wages are therefore low, he can save almost nothing on bread for the purchase of other articles.

The English workingmen have shown the English Free Traders that they are not the dupes of their illusions or of their lies; and if, in spite of this, the workers have made common cause with the manufacturers against the landlords, it is for the purpose of destroying the last remnant of feudalism, that henceforth they may have only one enemy to deal with. The workers have not miscalculated, for the landlords, in order to revenge themselves upon the manufacturers, have made common cause with the workers to carry the Ten Hours Bill, which the latter had been vainly demanding for thirty years, and which was passed immediately after the repeal of the Corn Laws.

When Dr. Bowring, at the Congress of Economists, drew from his pocket a long list to show how many head of cattle, how much ham, bacon, poultry, &c., is imported into England, to be consumed — as he asserted — by the workers, he unfortunately forgot to state that at the same time the workers of Manchester and other factory towns were thrown out of work by the beginning of the crisis.

As a matter of principle in Political Economy, the figures of a single year must never be taken as the basis for formulating general laws. We must always take the average of from six to seven years, a period during which modern industry passes through the successive phases of prosperity, over-production, crisis, thus completing the inevitable cycle.

Doubtless, if the price of all commodities falls,— and this is the necessary consequence of Free Trade,— I can buy far more for a franc than before. And the workingman's franc is as good as any other man's. There-

APPENDIX

fore, Free Trade must be advantageous to the workingman. There is only one little difficulty in this, namely, that the workman, before he exchanges his franc for other commodities, has first exchanged his labor for the money of the capitalist. If in this exchange he always received the said franc while the price of all other commodities fell he would always be the gainer by such a bargain. The difficulty does not lie in proving that, the price of all commodities falling, more commodities can be bought for the same sum of money.

Economists always take the price of labor at the moment of its exchange with other commodities, and altogether ignore the moment at which labor accomplishes its own exchange with capital. When it costs less to set in motion the machinery which produces commodities, then the things necessary for the maintenance of this machine, called workman, will also cost less. If all commodities are cheaper, labor, which is a commodity too, will also fall in price, and we shall see later that this commodity, labor, will fall far lower in proportion than all other commodities. If the workingman still pins his faith to the arguments of the economists, he will find, one fine morning, that the franc has dwindled in his pocket, and that he has only five sous left.

Thereupon the economist will tell you,—

"We admit that competition among the workers will certainly not be lessened under Free Trade, and will very soon bring wages into harmony with the low price of commodities. But, on the other hand, the low price of commodities will increase consumption, the larger consumption will increase production, which will in turn necessitate a larger demand for labor, and this larger demand will be followed by a rise in wages.

APPENDIX

"The whole argument amounts to this: Free Trade increases productive forces. When manufactures keep advancing, when wealth, when the productive forces, when, in a word, productive capital increases, the demand for labor, the price of labor, and consequently the rate of wages, rises also."

The most favorable condition for the workingman is the growth of capital. This must be admitted: when capital remains stationary, commerce and manufacture are not merely stationary but decline, and in this case the workman is the first victim. He will suffer before the capitalist. And in the case of the growth of capital, under the circumstances, which, as we have said, are the best for the workingman, what will be his lot? He will suffer just the same. The growth of capital implies the accumulation and the concentration of capital. This centralisation involves a greater division of labor and a greater use of machinery. The greater division of labor destroys the especial skill of the laborer; and by putting in the place of this skilled work labor which anyone can perform it increases competition among the workers.

This competition becomes more fierce as the division of labor enables a single man to do the work of three. Machinery accomplishes the same result on a much larger scale. The accumulation of productive capital forces the industrial capitalist to work with constantly increasing means of production, ruins the small manufacturer, and throws him into the ranks of the proletariat. Then, the rate of interest falling in proportion as capital accumulates, the people of small means and retired tradespeople, who can no longer live upon their small incomes, will be forced to look out for some business again and ultimately to swell the number of prole-

APPENDIX

tarians. Finally, the more productive capital grows, the more it is compelled to produce for a market whose requirements it does not know,—the more supply tries to force demand, and consequently crises increase in frequency and in intensity. But every crisis in turn hastens the concentration of capital, adds to the proletariat. Thus, as productive capital grows, competition among the workers grows too, and grows in a far greater proportion. The reward of labor is less for all, and the burden of labor is increased for at least some of them.

In 1829 there were, in Manchester, 1,088 cotton spinners employed in 36 factories. In 1841 there were but 448, and they tended 55,353 more spindles than the 1,088 spinners did in 1829. If manual labor had increased in the same proportion as productive force, the number of spinners ought to have risen to 1,848; improved machinery had, therefore, deprived 1,100 workers of employment.

We know beforehand the reply of the economists—the people thus thrown out of work will find other kinds of employment. Dr. Bowring did not fail to reproduce this argument at the Congress of Economists. But neither did he fail to refute himself. In 1833, Dr. Bowring made a speech in the House of Commons upon the 50,000 hand-loom weavers of London who have been starving without being able to find that new kind of employment which the Free Traders hold out to them in the distance. I will give the most striking portion of this speech of Mr. Bowring.

"The misery of the hand-loom weavers," he says, "is the inevitable fate of all kinds of labor which are easily acquired, and which may, at any moment, be replaced by less costly means. As in these cases competition

APPENDIX

amongst the workpeople is very great, the slightest falling-off in demand brings on a crisis. The hand-loom weavers are, in a certain sense, placed on the verge of human existence. One step further, and that existence becomes impossible. The slightest shock is sufficient to throw them on the road to ruin. By more and more superseding manual labor, the progress of mechanical science must result, during the period of transition, in much temporary suffering. National well-being cannot be bought except at the price of some individual evils. The advance of industry is achieved at the expense of those who lag behind, and of all discoveries that of the power-loom weighs most heavily upon the hand-loom weavers. In a great many articles formerly made by hand, the weaver has been completely ousted; but he is sure to be beaten in a good many more stuffs that are now made by hand."

Further on he says:—" I hold in my hand a correspondence of the Governor-General with the East India Company. This correspondence is concerning the weavers of the Dacca district. The Governor says in his letter:— A few years ago the East India Company received from six to eight million pieces of calico woven upon the looms of the country. The demand fell off gradually and was reduced to about a million pieces. At this moment it has almost entirely ceased. Moreover, in 1800, North America received from India nearly 800,000 pieces of cotton goods. In 1830 it did not take even 4,000. Finally, in 1800 a million of pieces were shipped to Portugal; in 1830 Portugal did not receive above 20,000.

" The reports on the distress of the Indian weavers are terrible. And what is the origin of that distress? The presence on the market of English manufactures,

APPENDIX

the production of the same article by means of the power-loom. A great number of the weavers died of starvation; the remainder has gone over to other employment, and chiefly to field labor. Not to be able to change employment amounted to a sentence of death. And at this moment the Dacca district is crammed with English yarns and piece goods. The Dacca muslin, renowned all over the world for its beauty and firm texture, has also been eclipsed by the competition of English machinery. In the whole history of commerce, it would, perhaps, be difficult to find suffering equal to what these whole classes in India had to submit to."

Mr. Bowring's speech is the more remarkable because the facts quoted by him are correct, and the phrases with which he seeks to palliate them are characterised by the hypocrisy common to all Free Trade discourses. He represents the workers as means of production which must be superseded by less expensive means of production, pretends to see in the labor of which he speaks a wholly exceptional kind of labor, and in the machine which has crushed out the weavers an equally exceptional kind of machine. He forgets that there is no kind of manual labor which may not any day share the fate of the hand-loom weavers.

"The constant aim and tendency of every improvement of mechanism is indeed to do entirely without the labor of men, or to reduce its price, by superseding the labor of the adult males by that of women and children, or the work of the skilled by that of the unskilled workman. In most of the throstle mills, spinning is now entirely done by girls of sixteen years and less. The introduction of the self-acting mule has caused the discharge of most of the (adult male) spinners, while the children and young persons have been kept on."

APPENDIX

The above words of the most enthusiastic of **Free Traders**, Dr. Ure, are calculated to complete the confessions of Dr. Bowring. Mr. Bowring speaks of certain individual evils, and, at the same time, says that these individual evils destroy whole classes; he speaks of the temporary sufferings during a transition period, and does not deny that these temporary evils have implied for the majority the transition from life to death, and for the rest a transition from a better to a worse condition. When he asserts, farther on, that the sufferings of the working class are inseparable from the progress of industry, and are necessary to the prosperity of the nation, he simply says that the prosperity of the bourgeois class involves, as a necessary condition, the suffering of the laboring class.

All the comfort which Mr. Bowring offers the workers who perish, and, indeed, the whole doctrine of compensation which the 'Free Traders propound, amounts to this,—

You thousands of workers who are perishing, do not despair! You can die with an easy conscience. Your class will not perish. It will always be numerous enough for the capitalist class to decimate it without fear of annihilating it. Besides, how could capital be usefully applied if it did not take care to keep up its exploitable material, *i.e.*, the working men, to be exploited over and over again?

But, then, why propound as a problem still to be solved the question: What influence will the adoption of Free Trade have upon the condition of the working class? All the laws formulated by the political economists from Quesnay to Ricardo, have been based upon the hypothesis that the trammels which still interfere with commercial freedom have disappeared. These

APPENDIX

laws are confirmed in proportion as Free Trade is adopted. The first of these laws is that competition reduces the price of every commodity to the minimum cost of production. Thus the minimum of wages is the natural price of labor. And what is the minimum of wages? Just so much as is required for production of the articles absolutely necessary for the maintenance of the worker, and for the continued existence more or less poorly of his class.

But do not imagine that the worker receives *only* this minimum wage, and still less that he *always* receives it. No, according to this law, the working class will sometimes be more fortunate, will sometimes receive something above the minimum, but this surplus will merely make up for the deficit which they will have received below the minimum in times of industrial depression. That is to say that within a given time which recurs periodically in the cycle which commerce and industry describe while passing through the successive phases of prosperity, over-production, stagnation, and crisis, when reckoning all that the working class has had above and below mere necessaries, we shall see that, after all, they have received neither more nor less than the minimum, *i.e.*, the working class will have maintained itself as a class after enduring any amount of misery and misfortune, and after leaving many corpses upon the industrial battle-field. But what of that? The class will still exist; nay, more, it will have increased.

But this is not all. The progress of industry creates less and less expensive means of subsistence. Thus spirits have taken the place of beer, cotton that of wool and linen, and potatoes that of bread.

Thus, as means are constantly being found for the maintenance of labor on cheaper and more wretched

APPENDIX

food, the minimum of wages is constantly sinking. If these wages began by letting the man work to live, they end by forcing him to live the life of a machine. His existence has no other value than that of a simple productive force, and the capitalist treats him accordingly. This law of the commodity labor, of the minimum of wages, will be confirmed in proportion as the supposition of the economists, Free Trade, becomes an actual fact. Thus, of two things one: either we must reject all political economy based upon the assumption of Free Trade, or we must admit that under this same Free Trade the whole severity of the economic laws will fall upon the workers.

To sum up, what is Free Trade under the present conditions of society? Freedom of Capital. When you have torn down the few national barriers which still restrict the free development of capital, you will merely have given it complete freedom of action. So long as the relation of wage-labor to capital is permitted to exist, no matter how favorable the conditions under which you accomplish the exchange of commodities, there will always be a class which exploits and a class which is exploited. It is really difficult to understand the presumption of the Free Traders who imagine that the more advantageous application of capital will abolish the antagonism between industrial capitalists and wage-workers. On the contrary. The only result will be that the antagonism of these two classes will stand out more clearly.

Let us assume for a moment that there are no more Corn Laws or national and municipal import duties; that in a word all the accidental circumstances which to-day the workingman may look upon as a cause of his miserable condition have vanished, and we shall have

APPENDIX

removed so many curtains that hide from his eyes his real enemy.

He will see that capital released from all trammels will make him no less a slave than capital trammelled by import duties.

Gentlemen! Do not be deluded by the abstract word Liberty! Whose Liberty? Not the liberty of one individual in relation to another, but the liberty of Capital to crush the worker.

Why should you desire farther to sanction unlimited competition with this idea of freedom, when the idea of freedom itself is only the product of a social condition based upon Free Competition?

We have shown what sort of fraternity Free Trade begets between the different classes of one and the same nation. The fraternity which Free Trade would establish between the nations of the earth would not be more real; to call cosmopolitan exploitation universal brotherhood is an idea that could only be engendered in the brain of the bourgeoisie. Every one of the destructive phenomena which unlimited competition gives rise to within any one nation is reproduced in more gigantic proportions in the market of the world. We need not pause any longer upon Free Trade sophisms on this subject, which are worth just as much as the arguments of our prize essayists, Messrs. Hope, Morse, and Greg.

For instance, we are told that Free Trade would create an international division of labor, and thereby give to each country those branches of production most in harmony with its natural advantages.

You believe, perhaps, gentlemen, that the production of coffee and sugar is the natural destiny of the West Indies.

Two centuries ago, nature, which does not trouble

APPENDIX

itself about commerce, had planted neither sugar-cane nor coffee trees there. And it may be that in less than half a century you will find there neither coffee nor sugar, for the East Indies, by means of cheaper production, have already successfully broken down this so-called natural destiny of the West Indies.

And the West Indies, with their natural wealth, are as heavy a burden for England as the weavers of Dacca, who also were destined from the beginning of time to weave by hand.

One other circumstance must not be forgotten, namely, that, just as everything has become a monopoly, there are also nowadays some branches of industry which prevail over all others, and secure to the nations which especially foster them the command of the world market. Thus in the commerce of the world cotton alone has much greater commercial importance than all the other raw materials used in the manufacture of clothing. It is indeed ridiculous for the Free Traders to refer to the few specialities in each branch of industry, throwing them into the scales against the products used in everyday consumption, and produced most cheaply in those countries in which manufacture is most highly developed.

If the Free Traders cannot understand how one nation can grow rich at the expense of another, we need not wonder, since these same gentlemen also refuse to understand how in the same country one class can enrich itself at the expense of another.

Do not imagine, gentlemen, that in criticising freedom of commerce we have the least intention of defending Protection.

One may be opposed to constitutionalism without being in favor of absolutism.

Moreover, the Protective system is nothing but a

APPENDIX

means of establishing manufacture upon a large scale in any given country, that is to say, of making it dependent upon the market of the world; and from the moment that dependence upon the market of the world is established, there is more or less dependence upon Free Trade too. Besides this, the Protective system helps to develop free competition within a nation. Hence we see that in countries where the bourgeoisie is beginning to make itself felt as a class, in Germany for example, it makes great efforts to obtain Protective duties. They serve the bourgeoisie as weapons against feudalism and absolute monarchy, as a means for the concentration of its own powers for the realisation of Free Trade within the country.

But generally speaking, the Free Trade system is destructive. It breaks up old nationalities and carries the antagonism between proletariat and bourgeoisie to the uttermost point. In a word, the system of commercial freedom hastens the Social Revolution. In this revolutionary sense alone, gentlemen, I am in favor of Free Trade.

THE END.